ACROSS MONGOLIAN PLAINS

A Naturalist's Account of
China's "Great Northwest"

By
Roy Chapman Andrews

*Associate Curator of Mammals in the
American Museum of Natural History,
And leader of the Museum's
Second Asiatic Expedition.
Author of "Whale Hunting with Gun and Camera,"
"Camps and Trails in China," etc.*

NATAL PUBLISHING LLC

ARS LONGA, VITA BREVIS

A NOMAD OF THE MONGOLIAN
PLAINS

PHOTOGRAPHS BY
YVETTE BORUP ANDREWS
Photographer of the
Second Asiatic Expedition

This book is affectionately dedicated to Dr. J.A. Allen who,
through his profound knowledge, unselfish devotion to
science, and never-failing sympathy with younger students
of zoology has been an example and an inspiration during
the years I have worked at his side.

PREFACE

During 1916-1917 the First Asiatic Expedition of the American Museum of Natural History carried on zoölogical explorations along the frontiers of Tibet and Burma in the little-known province of Yün-nan, China. The narrative of that expedition has already been given to the public in the first boot of this series "Camps and Trails in China." It was always the intention of the American Museum to continue the Asiatic investigations, and my presence in China on other work in 1918 gave the desired opportunity at the conclusion of the war.

Having made extensive collections along the southeastern edge of the great central Asian plateau, it was especially desirable to obtain a representation of the fauna from the northeastern part in preparation for the great expedition which, I am glad to say, is now in course of preparation, and which will conduct work in various other branches of science. Consequently, my wife and I spent one of the most delightful years of our lives in Mongolia and North China on the Second Asiatic Expedition of the American Museum of Natural History.

The present book is the narrative of our work and travels. As in "Camps and Trails" I have written it entirely from the sportsman's standpoint and have purposely avoided scientific details which would prove uninteresting or wearisome to the general public. Full reports of the expedition's results will appear in due course in the Museum's scientific publications and to them I would refer those readers who wish further details of the Mongolian fauna.

Asia is the most fascinating hunting ground in all the world, not because of the *quantity* of game to be found there but because of its *quality*, and scientific importance. Central Asia was the point of origin and distribution for many mammals which inhabit other parts of the earth to-day and the habits and relationships of some of its big game animals are almost unknown. Because of unceasing native persecution, lack of protection, the continued destruction of forests and the ever-increasing facilities for transportation to the remote districts of the interior, many of China's most interesting and important forms of wildlife are doomed to extermination in the very near future.

Fortunately world museums are awakening to the necessity of obtaining representative series of Asiatic mammals before it is too late, and to the broad vision of the President and Board of Trustees of the American Museum of Natural History my wife and I owe the exceptional opportunities which have been given us to carry on zoölogical explorations in Asia.

We are especially grateful to President Henry Fairfield Osborn, who is ready, always, to support enthusiastically any plans which tend to increase knowledge of China or to strengthen cordial relations between the United States and the Chinese Republic.

Director F. A. Lucas and Assistant Secretary George H. Sherwood have never failed in their attention to the needs of our expeditions when in the field and to them I extend our best thanks. Mr. and Mrs. Charles L. Bernheimer, who have contributed to every expedition in which I have taken part, generously rendered financial aid for the Mongolian work.

My wife, who is ever my best assistant in the field, was responsible for all the photographic work of the expedition and I have drawn much upon her daily "Journals" in the preparation of this book.

I wish to acknowledge the kindness of the Editors of *Harper's Magazine*, *Natural History*, *Asia Magazine* and the *Trans-Pacific Magazine* in whose publications parts of this book have already appeared.

We are indebted to a host of friends who gave assistance to the expedition and to us personally in the field: The Wai Chiao Pu (Ministry of Foreign Affairs) freely granted permits for the expedition to travel throughout China and extended other courtesies for which I wish to express appreciation on behalf of the President and Board of Trustees of the American Museum of Natural History.

In Peking, His Excellency Paul S. Reinsch, formerly American Minister to China, Dr. C. D. Tenney, Mr. Willys Peck, Mr. Ernest B. Price and other members of the Legation staff obtained import permits and attended to many details connected with the Chinese Government.

Mr. A. M. Guptil acted as our Peking representative while we were in the field and assumed much annoying detail in forwarding and receiving shipments of supplies and equipment. Other gentlemen in Peking who rendered us courtesies in various ways are Commanders I. V. Gillis and C. T. Hutchins, Dr. George D. Wilder, Dr. J. G. Anderson and Messrs. H. C. Faxon, E. G. Smith, C. R. Bennett, M. E. Weatherall and J. Kenrick.

In Kalgan, Mr. Charles L. Coltman arranged for the transportation of the expedition to Mongolia and not only gratuitously acted as our agent but was always ready to devote his own time and the use of his motor cars to further the work of the party.

In Urga, Mr. F. A. Larsen of Anderson, Meyer & Company, was of invaluable assistance in obtaining horses, carts and other equipment for the expedition as well as in giving us the benefit of his long and unique experience in Mongolia.

Mr. E. V. Olufsen of Anderson, Meyer & Company, put himself, his house, and his servants at our disposal whenever we were in Urga and aided us in innumerable ways.

Mr. and Mrs. Oscar Mamen often entertained us in their home. Mr. and Mrs. E. L. MacCallie, who accompanied us on one trip across Mongolia and later resided temporarily in Urga, brought equipment for us across Mongolia and entertained us while we were preparing to return to Peking.

Monsieur A. Orlow, Russian Diplomatic Agent in Urga, obtained permits from the Mongolian Government for our work in the Urga region and gave us much valuable advice.

In south China, Reverend H. Castle of Tunglu, and Reverend Lacy Moffet planned a delightful hunting trip for us in Che-kiang Province. In Shanghai the Hon. E. S. Cunningham, American Consul-General, materially aided the expedition in the shipment of specimens. To Mr. G. M. Jackson, General Passenger Agent of the Canadian Pacific Ocean Services, thanks are due for arranging for rapid transportation to America of our valuable collections.

ROY CHAPMAN ANDREWS
AMERICAN MUSEUM OF NATURAL HISTORY,
NEW YORK CITY, U. S. A.

CONTENTS

CHAPTER XVIII
WILD PIGS ANIMAL AND HUMAN

Shansi Province famous for wild boar—Flesh delicious—When to hunt—Where to go—Inns and coal gas—Kaochia-chuang—A long shot—Our camp at Tziloa—Native hunters—A young pig—A hard chase—Pheasants—Another pig—Smith runs down a big sow—Chinese steal our game—A wounded boar

CHAPTER XIX
THE HUNTING PARK OF THE EASTERN TOMBS

A visit to Duke Tsai Tse—A "personality"—The *Tung Ling*—The road to the tombs—A country inn—The front view of the *Tung Ling*—The tombs of the Empress Dowager and Ch'ien Lung—The "hinterland"—An area of desolation—Our camp in the forest—Reeves's pheasant—The most beautiful Chinese deer—"Blood horns" as medicine—Goral—Animals and birds of the *Tung Ling*—A new method of catching trout—A forest fire—Native stupidity—Wanton destruction—China's great opportunity

Index

ILLUSTRATIONS

INTRODUCTION

The romantic story of the Mongols and their achievements has been written so completely that it is unnecessary to repeat it here even though it is as fascinating as a tale from the *Arabian Nights*. The present status of the country, however, is but little known to the western world. In a few words I will endeavor to sketch the recent political developments, some of which occurred while we were in Mongolia.

In the twelfth and thirteenth centuries the great Genghiz Khan and his illustrious successor Kublai Khan "almost in a night" erected the greatest empire the world has ever seen. Not only did they conquer all of Asia, but they advanced in Europe as far as the Dnieper leaving behind a trail of blood and slaughter.

All Europe rose against them, but what could not be accomplished by force of arms was wrought in the Mongols themselves by an excess of luxury. In their victorious advance great stores of treasure fell into their hands and they gave themselves to a life of ease and indulgence.

By nature the Mongols were hard riding, hard living warriors, accustomed to privation and fatigue. The poison of luxury ate into the very fibers of their being and gradually they lost the characteristics which had made them great. The ruin of the race was completed by the introduction of Lamaism, a religion which carries only moral destruction where it enters, and eventually the Mongols passed under the rule of the once conquered Chinese and then under the Manchus.

Until the overthrow of the Manchu regime in China in 1911, and the establishment of the present republic, there were no particularly significant events in Mongolian history. But at that time the Russians, wishing to create a buffer state between themselves and China as well as to obtain special commercial privileges in Mongolia, aided the Mongols in rebellion, furnished them with arms and ammunition and with officers to train their men.

A somewhat tentative proclamation of independence for Outer Mongolia was issued in December, 1911, by the

Hutukhtu and nobles of Urga, and the Chinese were driven out of the country with little difficulty. Beset with internal troubles, the Chinese paid but scant attention to Mongolian affairs until news was received in Peking in October, 1912, that M. Korostovetz, formerly Russian Minister to China, had arrived secretly in Urga and on November 3, 1912, had recognized the independence of Outer Mongolia on behalf of his Government.

It then became incumbent upon China to take official note of the situation, especially as foreign complications could not be faced in view of her domestic embarrassments.

Consequently on November 5, 1913, there was concluded a Russo-Chinese agreement wherein Russia recognized that Outer Mongolia was under the suzerainty of China, and China, on her part, admitted the autonomy of Outer Mongolia. The essential element in the situation was the fact that Russia stood behind the Mongols with money and arms and China's hand was forced at a time when she was powerless to resist.

Quite naturally, Mongolia's political status has been a sore point with China and it is hardly surprising that she should have awaited an opportunity to reclaim what she considered to be her own.

This opportunity arrived with the collapse of Russia and the spread of Bolshevism, for the Mongols were dependent upon Russia for material assistance in anything resembling military operations, although, as early as 1914, they had begun to realize that they were cultivating a dangerous friend. The Mongolian army, at the most, numbered only two or three thousand poorly equipped and undisciplined troops who would require money and organization before they could become an effective fighting force.

The Chinese were not slow to appreciate these conditions and General Hsu Shu-tseng, popularly known as "Little Hsu," by a clever bit of Oriental intrigue sent four thousand soldiers to Urga with the excuse of protecting the Mongols from a so-called threatened invasion of Buriats and brigands. A little later he himself arrived in a motor car and, when the stage was set, brought such pressure to bear upon the Hutukhtu and his Cabinet that they had no recourse except to cancel

Mongolia's autonomy and ask to return to their former place under Chinese rule.

This they did on November 17, 1919, in a formal Memorial addressed to the President of the Chinese Republic, which is quoted below as it appeared in the Peking press, under date of November 24, 1919:

"We, the Ministers and Vice-Ministers [here follow their names and ranks] of all the departments of the autonomous Government of Outer Mongolia, and all the princes, dukes, hutukhtus and lamas and others resident at Urga, hereby jointly and severally submit the following petition for the esteemed perusal of His Excellency the President of the Republic of China:—

"Outer Mongolia has been a dependency of China since the reign of the Emperor Kang Hsi, remaining loyal for over two hundred years, the entire population, from princes and dukes down to the common people having enjoyed the blessings of peace. During the reign of the Emperor Tao Kwang changes in the established institutions, which were opposed to Mongolian sentiment, caused dissatisfaction which was aggravated by the corruption of the administration during the last days of the Manchu Dynasty. Taking advantage of this Mongolian dissatisfaction, foreigners instigated and assisted the independence movement. Upon the Kiakhta Convention, being signed the autonomy of Outer Mongolia was held a *fait accompli*, China retaining an empty suzerainty while the officials and people of Outer Mongolia lost many of their old rights and privileges. Since the establishment of this autonomous government no progress whatsoever has been chronicled, the affairs of government being indeed plunged in a state of chaos, causing deep pessimism.

"Lately, chaotic conditions have also reigned supreme in Russia, reports of revolutionary elements threatening our frontiers having been frequently received. Moreover, since the Russians have no united government it is only natural that they are powerless to carry out the provisions of the treaties, and now that they have no control over their subjects the Buriat tribes have constantly conspired and cooperated with bandits, and repeatedly sent delegates to Urga urging our

Government to join with them and form a Pan-Mongolian nation. That this propaganda work, so varied and so persistent, which aims at usurping Chinese suzerainty and undermining the autonomy of Outer Mongolia, does more harm than good to Outer Mongolia, our Government is well aware. The Buriats, with their bandit Allies, now considering us unwilling to espouse their cause, contemplate dispatching troops to violate our frontiers and to compel our submission. Furthermore, forces from the so-called White Army have forcibly occupied Tanu Ulianghai, an old possession of Outer Mongolia, and attacked both Chinese and Mongolian troops, this being followed by the entry of the Red Army, thus making the situation impossible.

"Now that both our internal and external affairs have reached such a climax, we, the members of the Government, in view of the present situation, have assembled all the princes, dukes, lamas and others and have held frequent meetings to discuss the question of our future welfare. Those present have been unanimously of the opinion that the old bonds of friendship having been restored our autonomy should be canceled, since Chinese and Mongolians are filled with a common purpose and ideal.

"The result of our decision has been duly reported to His Holiness the Bogdo Jetsun Dampa Hutukhtu Khan and has received his approval and support. Such being the position we now unanimously petition His Excellency the President that the old order of affairs be restored."

(Signed)

"Premier and Acting Minister of the Interior, Prince Lama Batma Torgoo.

Vice-Minister, Prince of Tarkhan Puntzuk Cheilin.

Vice-Minister, Great Lama of Beliktu, Prince Puntzuk Torgoo.

Minister of Foreign Affairs, Duke Cheilin Torgoo.

Vice-Minister, Dalai Prince Cheitantnun Lomour.

Vice-Minister, Prince of Ochi, Kaotzuktanba.

Minister of War, Prince of Eltoni Jamuyen Torgoo.

Vice-Minister, Prince of Eltoni Selunto Chihloh.

Vice-Minister, Prince of Elteni Punktzu Laptan.

Vice-Minister, Prince of Itkemur Chitu Wachir.

Minister of Finance, Prince Lama Loobitsan Paletan.
Vice-Minister, Prince Torgee Cheilin.
Vice-Minister, Prince of Suchuketu Tehmutgu Kejwan.
Minister of Justice, Dalai of Chiechenkhan Wananin.
Vice-Minister, Prince of Daichinchihlun Chackehbatehorhu.
Vice-Minister, Prince of Cholikota Lama Dashtunyupu,"

Naturally, the President of China graciously consented to allow the prodigal to return and "killed the fatted calf" by conferring high honors and titles upon the Hutukhtu. Moreover, he appointed the Living Buddha's good friend (?) "Little Hsu" to convey them to him.

Thus, Mongolia again has become a part of China. Who knows what the future has in store for her? But events are moving rapidly and by the time this book is published the curtain may have risen upon a new act of Mongolia's tragedy.

CHAPTER I
ENTERING THE LAND OF MYSTERY

Careering madly in a motor car behind a herd of antelope fleeing like wind-blown ribbons across a desert which isn't a desert, past caravans of camels led by picturesque Mongol horsemen, the Twentieth Century suddenly and violently interjected into the Middle Ages, should be contrast and paradox enough for even the most blasé sportsman. I am a naturalist who has wandered into many of the far corners of the earth. I have seen strange men and things, but what I saw on the great Mongolian plateau fairly took my breath away and left me dazed, utterly unable to adjust my mental perspective.

When leaving Peking in late August, 1918, to cross the Gobi Desert in Mongolia, I knew that I was to go by motor car. But somehow the very names "Mongolia" and "Gobi Desert" brought such a vivid picture of the days of Kublai Khan and ancient Cathay that my clouded mind refused to admit the thought of automobiles. It was enough that I was going to the land of which I had so often dreamed.

Not even in the railway, when I was being borne toward Kalgan and saw lines of laden camels plodding silently along the paved road beside the train, or when we puffed slowly through the famous Nankou Pass and I saw that wonder of the world, the Great Wall, winding like a gray serpent over ridge after ridge of the mountains, was my dream-picture of mysterious Mongolia dispelled. I had seen all this before, and had accepted it as one accepts the motor cars beside the splendid walls of old Peking. It was too near, and the railroad had made it commonplace.

But Mongolia! That was different. One could not go there in a roaring train. I had beside me the same old rifle and sleeping bag that had been carried across the mountains of far Yün-nan, along the Tibetan frontier, and through the fever-stricken jungles of Burma. Somehow, these companions of forest and mountain trails, and my reception at Kalgan by two khaki-clad young men, each with a belt of cartridges and a six-shooter strapped about his waist, did much to keep me in a blissful state of unpreparedness for the destruction of my dream-castles.

That night as we sat in Mr. Charles Coltman's home, with his charming wife, a real woman of the great outdoors, presiding at the dinner table, the talk was all of shooting, horses, and the vast, lone spaces of the Gobi Desert—but not much of motor cars. Perhaps they vaguely realized that I was still asleep in an unreal world and knew that the awakening would come all too soon.

Yet I was dining that night with one of the men who had destroyed the mystery of Mongolia. In 1916, Coltman and his former partner, Oscar Mamen, had driven across the plains to Urga, the historic capital of Mongolia. But most unromantic and incongruous, most disheartening to a dreamer of Oriental dreams, was what I learned a few days later when the awakening had really come—that among the first cars ever to cross the desert was one purchased by the Hutukhtu, the Living Buddha, the God of all the Mongols.

When the Hutukhtu learned of the first motor car in Mongolia he forthwith demanded one for himself. So his automobile was brought safely through the rocky pass at Kalgan and across the seven hundred miles of plain to Urga by way of the same old caravan trail over which, centuries ago, Genghis Khan had sent his wild Mongol raiders to conquer China.

We arose long before daylight on the morning of August 29. In the courtyard lanterns flashed and disappeared like giant fireflies as the *mafus* (muleteers) packed the baggage and saddled the ponies. The cars had been left on the plateau at a mission station called Hei-ma-hou to avoid the rough going in the pass, and we were to ride there on horseback while the food and bed-rolls went by cart. There were five of us in the party—Mr. and Mrs. Coltman, Mr. and Mrs. Lucander, and myself. I was on a reconnaissance and Mr. Coltman's object was to visit his trading station in Urga, where the Lucanders were to remain for the winter.

The sun was an hour high when we clattered over the slippery paving stones to the north gate of the city. Kalgan is built hard against the Great Wall of China—the first line of defense, the outermost rampart in the colossal structure which for so many centuries protected China from Tartar invasion. Beyond it there was nothing between us and the great plateau.

After our passports had been examined we rode through the gloomy chasm-like gate, turned sharply to the left, and found ourselves standing on the edge of a half-dry river bed. Below us stretched line after line of double-humped camels, some crowded in yellow-brown masses which seemed all heads and curving necks, and some kneeling quietly on the sand. From around a shoulder of rock came other camels, hundreds of them, treading slowly and sedately, nose to tail, toward the gate in the Great Wall. They had come from the far country whither we were bound. To me there is something fascinating about a camel. Perhaps it is because he seems to typify the great waste spaces which I love, that I never tire of watching him swing silently, and seemingly with resistless power, across the desert.

Our way to Hei-ma-hou led up the dry river bed, with the Great Wall on the left stretching its serpentine length across the hills, and on the right picturesque cliffs two hundred feet in height. At their bases nestle mud-roofed cottages and Chinese inns, but farther up the river the low hills are all of *loess*—brown, wind-blown dust, packed hard, which can be cut like cheese. Deserted though they seem from a distance, they really teem with human life. Whole villages are half dug, half built, into the hillsides, but are well-nigh invisible, for every wall and roof is of the same brown earth.

Ten miles or so from Kalgan we began on foot the long climb up the pass which gives entrance to the great plateau. I kept my eyes steadily on the pony's heels until we reached a broad, flat terrace halfway up the pass. Then I swung about that I might have, all at once, the view which lay below us. It justified my greatest hopes, for miles and miles of rolling hills stretched away to where the far horizon met the Shansi Mountains.

It was a desolate country which I saw, for every wave in this vast land-sea was cut and slashed by the knives of wind and frost and rain, and lay in a chaotic mass of gaping wounds—cañons, ravines, and gullies, painted in rainbow colors, crossing and cutting one another at fantastic angles as far as the eye could see.

When, a few moments later, we reached the very summit of the pass, I felt that no spot I had ever visited satisfied my preconceived conceptions quite so thoroughly. Behind and below us lay that stupendous relief map of ravines and gorges; in front was a limitless stretch of undulating plain, I knew then that I really stood upon the edge of the greatest plateau in all the world and that it could be only Mongolia.

We had tiffin at a tiny Chinese inn beside the road, and trotted on toward Hei-ma-hou between waving fields of wheat, buckwheat, millet, and oats—oats as thick and "meaty" as any horse could wish to eat.

After tiffin Coltman and Lucander rode rapidly ahead while I trotted my pony along more slowly in the rear. It was nearly seven o'clock, and the trees about the mission station had been visible for half an hour. I was enjoying a gorgeous sunset which splashed the western sky with gold and red, and lazily watching the black silhouettes of a camel caravan swinging along the summit of a ridge a mile away. On the road beside me a train of laden mules and bullock-carts rested for a moment—the drivers half asleep. Over all the plain there lay the peace of a perfect autumn evening.

Suddenly, from behind a little rise, I heard the whir of a motor engine and the raucous voice of a Klaxon horn. Before I realized what it meant, I was in the midst of a mass of plunging, snorting animals, shouting carters, and kicking mules. In a moment the caravan scattered wildly across the plain and the road was clear save for the author of the turmoil—a black automobile.

I wish I could make those who spend their lives within a city know how strange and out of place that motor seemed, alone there upon the open plain on the borders of Mongolia. Imagine a camel or an elephant with all its Oriental trappings suddenly appearing on Fifth Avenue! You would think at once that it had escaped from a circus or a zoo and would be mainly curious as to what the traffic policeman would do when it did not obey his signals.

But all the incongruity and the fact that the automobile was a glaring anachronism did not prevent my abandoning my horse to the *mafu* and stretching out comfortably on the cushions of the rear seat. There I had nothing to do but collect the remains of my shattered dream-castles as we bounced over the ruts and stones. It was a rude awakening, and I felt half ashamed to admit to myself as the miles sped by that the springy seat was more comfortable than the saddle on my Mongol pony.

But that night when I strolled about the mission courtyard, under the spell of the starry, desert sky, I drifted back again in thought to the glorious days of Kublai Khan. My heart was hot with resentment that this thing had come. I realized then that, for better or for worse, the sanctity of the desert was gone forever. Camels will still plod their silent way across the age-old plains, but the mystery is lost. The secrets which were yielded up to but a chosen few are open now to all, and the world and his wife will speed their noisy course across the miles of rolling prairie, hearing nothing, feeling nothing, knowing nothing of that resistless desert charm which led men out into the Great Unknown.

At daylight we packed the cars. Bed-rolls and cans of gasoline were tied on the running boards and every corner was filled with food. Our rifles were ready for use, however, for Coltman had promised a kind of shooting such as I had never seen before. The stories he told of wild rides in the car after strings of antelope which traveled at fifty or sixty miles an hour had left me mildly skeptical. But then, you know, I had never seen a Mongolian antelope run.

For twenty or thirty miles after leaving Hei-ma-hou we bounced along over a road which would have been splendid except for the deep ruts cut by mule- and ox-carts. These carts are the despair of any one who hopes some time to see good roads in China. The spike-studded wheels cut into the hardest ground and leave a chaos of ridges and chasms which grows worse with every year.

We were seldom out of sight of mud-walled huts or tiny Chinese villages, and Chinese peddlers passed our cars, carrying baskets of fruit or trinkets for the women. Chinese farmers stopped to gaze at us as we bounded over the ruts— in fact it was all Chinese, although we were really in Mongolia. I was very eager to see Mongols, to register first impressions of a people of whom I had dreamed so much; but the blue-clad Chinaman was ubiquitous.

PLATE I

Roy Chapman Andrews on "Kublai Khan"

Yvette Borup Andrews, Photographer of the Expedition

For seventy miles from Kalgan it was all the same—
Chinese everywhere. The Great Wall was built to keep the
Mongols out, and by the same token it should have kept the
Chinese in. But the rolling, grassy sea of the vast plateau was
too strong a temptation for the Chinese farmer. Encouraged
by his own government, which knows the value of just such
peaceful penetration, he pushes forward the line of
cultivation a dozen miles or so every year. As a result the

grassy hills have given place to fields of wheat, oats, millet, buckwheat, and potatoes.

The Mongol, above all things, is not a farmer; possibly because, many years ago, the Manchus forbade him to till the soil. Moreover, on the ground he is as awkward as a duck out of water and he is never comfortable. The back of a pony is his real home, and he will do wonderfully well any work which keeps him in the saddle. As Mr. F. A. Larsen in Urga once said, "A Mongol would make a splendid cook if you could give him a horse to ride about on in the kitchen." So he leaves to the plodding Chinaman the cultivation of his boundless plains, while he herds his fat-tailed sheep and goats and cattle.

About two hours after leaving the mission station we passed the limit of cultivation and were riding toward the Tabool hills. There Mr. Larsen, the best known foreigner in all Mongolia, has a home, and as we swung past the trail which leads to his house we saw one of his great herds of horses grazing in the distance.

All the land in this region has long, rich grass in summer, and water is by no means scarce. There are frequent wells and streams along the road, and in the distance we often caught a glint of silver from the surface of a pond or lake. Flocks of goats and fat-tailed sheep drifted up the valley, and now and then a herd of cattle massed themselves in moving patches on the hillsides. But they are only a fraction of the numbers which this land could easily support.

Not far from Tabool is a Mongol village. I jumped out of the car to take a photograph but scrambled in again almost as quickly, for as soon as the motor had stopped a dozen dogs dashed from the houses snarling and barking like a pack of wolves. They are huge brutes, these Mongol dogs, and as fierce as they are big. Every family and every caravan owns one or more, and we learned very soon never to approach a native encampment on foot.

The village was as unlike a Chinese settlement as it well could be, for instead of closely packed mud houses there were circular, latticed frameworks covered with felt and cone-shaped in the upper half. The *yurt*, as it is called, is perfectly adapted to the Mongols and their life. In the winter a stove is placed in the center, and the house is dry and warm. In the summer the felt covering is sometimes replaced by canvas which can be lifted on any side to allow free passage of air. When it is time for the semiannual migration to new grazing grounds the *yurt* can be quickly dismantled, the framework collapsed, and the house packed on camels or carts.

The Mongols of the village were rather disappointing, for many of them show a strong element of Chinese blood. This seems to have developed an unfortunate combination of the worst characteristics of both races. Even where there is no real mixture, their contact with the Chinese has been demoralizing, and they will rob and steal at every opportunity. The headdresses of the southern women are by no means as elaborate as those in the north.

When the hills of Tabool had begun to sink on the horizon behind us, we entered upon a vast rolling plain, where there was but little water and not a sign of human life. It resembled nothing so much as the prairies of Nebraska or Dakota, and amid the short grass larkspur and purple thistles glowed in the sunlight like tongues of flame.

There was no lack of birds. In the ponds which we passed earlier in the day we saw hundreds of mallard ducks and teal. The car often frightened golden plover from their dust baths in the road, and crested lapwings flashed across the prairie like sudden storms of autumn leaves. Huge, golden eagles and enormous ravens made tempting targets on the telegraph poles, and in the morning before we left the cultivated area we saw demoiselle cranes in thousands.

In this land where wood is absent and everything that will make a fire is of value, I wondered how it happened that the telegraph poles remained untouched, for every one was smooth and round without a splinter gone. The method of protection is simple and entirely Oriental. When the line was first erected, the Mongolian government stated in an edict that any man who touched a pole with knife or ax would lose his head. Even on the plains the enforcement of such a law is not so difficult as it might seem, and after a few heads had been taken by way of example the safety of the line was assured.

Our camp the first night was on a hill slope about one

hundred miles from Hei-ma-hou. As soon as the cars had stopped, one man was left to untie the sleeping bags while the rest of us scattered over the plain to hunt material for a fire. *Argul* (dried dung) forms the only desert fuel and, although it does not blaze like wood, it will "boil a pot" almost as quickly as charcoal. I was elected to be the cook—a position with distinct advantages, for in the freezing cold of early morning I could linger about the fire with a good excuse.

It was a perfect autumn night. Every star in the world of space seemed to have been crowded into our own particular expanse of sky, and each one glowed like a tiny lantern. When I had found a patch of sand and had dug a trench for my hip and shoulder, I crawled into the sleeping bag and lay for half an hour looking up at the bespangled canopy above my head. Again the magic of the desert night was in my blood, and I blessed the fate which had carried me away from the roar and rush of New York with its hurrying crowds. But I felt a pang of envy when, far away in the distance, there came the mellow notes of a camel-bell. *Dong, dong, dong* it sounded, clear and sweet as cathedral chimes. With surging blood I listened until I caught the measured tread of padded feet, and saw the black silhouettes of rounded bodies and curving necks. Oh, to be with them, to travel as Marco Polo traveled, and to learn to know the heart of the desert in the long night marches! Before I closed my eyes that night I vowed that when the war was done and I was free to travel where I willed, I would come again to the desert as the great Venetian came.

CHAPTER II
SPEED MARVELS OF THE GOBI DESERT

The next morning, ten miles from camp, we passed a party of Russians en route to Kalgan. They were sitting disconsolately beside two huge cars, patching tires and tightening bolts. Their way had been marked by a succession of motor troubles and they were almost discouraged. Woe to the men who venture into the desert with an untried car and without a skilled mechanic! There are no garages just around the corner—and there are no corners. Lucander's Chinese boy expressed it with laconic completeness when some one asked him how he liked the country.

"Well," said he, "there's plenty of *room*, here."

A short distance farther on we found the caravan which had passed us early in the night. They were camped beside a well and the thirsty camels were gorging themselves with water. Except for these wells, the march across the desert would be impossible. They are four or five feet wide, walled with timbers, and partly roofed. In some the water is rather brackish but always cool, for it is seldom less than ten feet below the surface. It is useless to speculate as to who dug the wells or when, for this trail has been used for centuries. In some regions they are fifty or even sixty miles apart, but usually less than that.

The camel caravans travel mostly at night. For all his size and apparent strength, a camel is a delicate animal and needs careful handling. He cannot stand the heat of the midday sun and he will not graze at night. So the Gobi caravans start about three or four o'clock in the afternoon and march until one or two the next morning. Then the men pitch a light tent and the camels sleep or wander over the plain.

At noon on the second day we reached Panj-kiang, the first telegraph station on the line. Its single mud house was visible miles away and we were glad to see it, for our gasoline was getting low. Coltman had sent a plentiful supply by caravan to await us here, and every available inch of space was filled with cans, for we were only one-quarter of the way to Urga.

Not far beyond Panj-kiang, a lama monastery has been

built beside the road. Its white-walled temple bordered with red and the compound enclosing the living quarters of the lamas show with startling distinctness on the open plain. We stopped for water at a well a few hundred yards away, and in five minutes the cars were surrounded by a picturesque group of lamas who streamed across the plain on foot and on horseback, their yellow and red robes flaming in the sun. They were amiable enough—in fact, too friendly—and their curiosity was hardly welcome, for we found one of them testing his knife on the tires and another about to punch a hole in one of the gasoline cans; he hoped it held something to drink that was better than water.

Thus far the trail had not been bad, as roads go in the Gobi, but I was assured that the next hundred miles would be a different story, for we were about to enter the most arid part of the desert between Kalgan and Urga. We were prepared for the only real work of the trip, however, by a taste of the exciting shooting which Coltman had promised me.

I had been told that we should see antelope in thousands, but all day I had vainly searched the plains for a sign of game. Ten miles from Panj-kiang we were rolling comfortably along on a stretch of good road when Mrs. Coltman, whose eyes are as keen as those of a hawk, excitedly pointed to a knoll on the right, not a hundred yards from the trail. At first I saw nothing but yellow grass; then the whole hillside seemed to be in motion. A moment later I began to distinguish heads and legs and realized that I was looking at an enormous herd of antelope, closely packed together, restlessly watching us.

Our rifles were out in an instant and Coltman opened the throttle. The antelope were five or six hundred yards away, and as the car leaped forward they ranged themselves in single file and strung out across the plain. We left the road at once and headed diagonally toward them. For some strange reason, when a horse or car runs parallel with a herd of antelope, the animals will swing in a complete semicircle and cross in front of the pursuer. This is also true of some African species. Whether they think they are being cut off from some more desirable means of escape I cannot say, but the fact remains that with the open plain on every side they always try to "cross your bows."

I shall never forget the sight of those magnificent animals streaming across the desert! There were at least a thousand of them, and their yellow bodies seemed fairly to skim the earth. I was shouting in excitement, but Coltman said:

"They're not running yet. Wait till we begin to shoot."

I could hardly believe my eyes when I saw the speedometer trembling at thirty-five miles, for we were making a poor showing with the antelope. But then the fatal attraction began to assert itself and the long column bent gradually in our direction. Coltman widened the arc of the circle and held the throttle up as far as it would go. Our speed increased to forty miles and the car began to gain because the antelope were running almost across our course.

They were about two hundred yards away when Coltman shut off the gas and jammed both brakes, but before the car had stopped they had gained another hundred. I leaped over a pile of bedding and came into action with the .250 Savage high-power as soon as my feet were on the ground. Coltman's .30 Mauser was already spitting fire from the front seat across the wind-shield, and at his second shot an antelope dropped like lead. My first two bullets struck the dirt far behind the rearmost animal, but the third caught a full-grown female in the side and she plunged forward into the grass.

I realized then what Coltman meant when he said that the antelope had not begun to run. At the first shot every animal in the herd seemed to flatten itself and settle to its work. They did not run—they simply *flew* across the ground, their legs showing only as a blur. The one I killed was four hundred yards away, and I held four feet ahead when I pulled the trigger. They could not have been traveling less than fifty-five or sixty miles an hour, for they were running in a semicircle about the car while we were moving at forty miles in a straight line.

Those are the facts in the case. I can see my readers raise their brows incredulously, for that is exactly what I would have done before this demonstration. Well, there is one way to prove it and that is to come and try it for yourselves. Moreover, I can see some sportsmen smile for another reason. I mentioned that the antelope I killed was four hundred yards away. I know how far it was, for I paced it off. I may say, in passing, that I had never before killed a running animal at that range. Ninety per cent of my shooting had been well within one hundred and fifty yards, but in Mongolia conditions are most extraordinary.

In the brilliant atmosphere an antelope at four hundred yards appears as large as it would at one hundred in most other parts of the world; and on the flat plains, where there is not a bush or a shrub to obscure the view, a tiny stone stands out like a golf ball on the putting green. Because of these conditions there is strong temptation to shoot at impossible ranges and to keep on shooting when the game is beyond anything except a lucky chance. Therefore, if any of you go to Mongolia to hunt antelope take plenty of ammunition, and when you return you will never tell how many cartridges you used. Our antelope were tied on the running board of the car and we went back to the road where Lucander was waiting. Half the herd had crossed in front of him, but he had failed to bring down an animal.

When the excitement was over I began to understand the significance of what we had seen. It was slowly borne in upon me that our car had been going, by the speedometer, at forty miles an hour and that the *antelope were actually beating us*. It was an amazing discovery, for I had never dreamed that any living animal could run so fast. It was a discovery, too, which would have important results, for Professor Henry Fairfield Osborn, president of the American Museum of Natural History, even then was carrying on investigations as to the relation of speed to limb structure in various groups of animals. I determined, with Mr. Coltman's help, to get some real facts in the case—data upon which we could rely.

There was an opportunity only to begin the study on the first trip, but we carried it further the following year. Time after time, as we tore madly after antelope, singly or in herds, I kept my eyes upon the speedometer, and I feel confident that our observations can be relied upon. We demonstrated beyond a doubt that the Mongolian antelope can reach a speed of from fifty-five to sixty miles an hour. This is probably the maximum *which is attained only in the initial sprint* and after a very short distance the animals must slow down to about forty miles; a short distance more and they drop to twenty-five or thirty miles, and at this pace they seem able to continue almost indefinitely. They never ran faster than was necessary to keep well away from us. As we opened the throttle of the car they, too, increased their speed. It was only when we began to shoot and they became thoroughly frightened that they showed what they could do.

I remember especially one fine buck which gave us an exhibition of really high-class running. He started almost opposite to us when we were on a stretch of splendid road and jogged comfortably along at thirty-five miles an hour. Our car was running at the same speed, but he decided to cross in front and pressed his accelerator a little. Coltman also touched ours, and the motor jumped to forty miles. The antelope seemed very much surprised and gave his accelerator another push. Coltman did likewise, and the speedometer registered forty-five miles. That was about enough for us, and we held our speed. The animal drew ahead on a long curve swinging across in front of the car. He had beaten us by a hundred yards!

But we had a surprise in store for him, for Coltman suddenly shut off the gas and threw on both brakes. Before the motor had fully stopped we opened fire. The first two bullets struck just behind the antelope and a third kicked the dust between his legs. The shock turned him half over, but he righted himself and ran to his very limit. The bullets spattering all about kept him at it for six hundred yards. He put up a desert hare on the way, but that hare didn't have a chance with the antelope. It reminded me of the story of the negro who had seen a ghost. He ran until he dropped beside the road, but the ghost was right beside him. "Well," said the ghost, "that was *some* race we had." "Yes," answered the negro, "but it ain't nothin' to what we're goin' to have soon's ever I git my breath. And then," said the negro, "we ran agin. And I come to a rabbit leggin' it up the road, and I said, 'Git out of the way, rabbit, and let some one run what *can* run!'" The last we saw of the antelope was a cloud of yellow dust disappearing over a low rise.

The excitement of the chase had been an excellent preparation for the hard work which awaited us not far ahead.

The going had been getting heavier with every mile, and at last we reached a long stretch of sandy road which the motors could not pull through. With every one except the driver out of the car, and the engine racing, we pushed and lifted, gaining a few feet each time, until the shifting sand was passed. It meant two hours of violent strain, and we were well-nigh exhausted; a few miles farther, however, it had all to be done again. Where the ground was hard, there was such a chaos of ruts and holes that our arms were almost wrenched from their sockets by the twisting wheels.

PLATE II

At the end of the long trail from outer Mongolia

Women of southern Mongolia

This area more nearly approaches a desert than any other part of the road to Urga. The soil is mainly sandy, but the Gobi sagebrush and short bunch grass, although sparse and dry, still give a covering of vegetation, so that in the distance the plain appears like a rolling meadowland.

When we saw our first northern Mongol I was delighted. Every one is a study for an artist. He dresses in a long, loose robe of plum color, one corner of which is usually tucked into a gorgeous sash. On his head is perched an extraordinary hat which looks like a saucer, with upturned edges of black velvet and a narrow cone-shaped crown of brilliant yellow. Two streamers of red ribbon are usually fastened to the rim at the back, or a plume of peacock feathers if he be of higher rank.

On his feet he wears a pair of enormous leather boots with pointed toes. These are always many sizes too large, for as the weather grows colder he pads them out with heavy socks of wool or fur. It is nearly impossible for him to walk in this ungainly footgear, and he waddles along exactly like a duck. He is manifestly uncomfortable and ill at ease, but put him on a horse and you have a different picture. The high-peaked saddle and the horse itself become a part of his anatomy and he will stay there happily fifteen hours of the day.

The Mongols ride with short stirrups and, standing nearly upright, lean far over the horse's neck like our western cowboys. As they tear along at full gallop in their brilliant robes they seem to embody the very spirit of the plains. They are such genial, accommodating fellows, always ready with a pleasant smile, and willing to take a sporting chance on anything under the sun, that they won my heart at once.

Above all things they love a race, and often one of them would range up beside the car and, with a radiant smile, make signs that he wished to test our speed. Then off he would go like mad, flogging his horse and yelling with delight. We would let him gain at first, and the expression of joy and triumph on his face was worth going far to see. Sometimes, if the road was heavy, it would need every ounce of gas the car could take to forge ahead, for the ponies are splendid animals. The Mongols ride only the best and ride them hard, since horses are cheap in Mongolia, and when one is a little worn another is always ready.

Not only does the Mongol inspire you with admiration for his full-blooded, virile manhood, but also you like him because he likes you. He doesn't try to disguise the fact. There is a frank openness about his attitude which is wonderfully appealing, and I believe that the average white man can get on terms of easy familiarity, and even intimacy, with Mongols more rapidly than with any other Orientals.

Ude is the second telegraph station on the road to Urga. It has the honor of appearing on most maps of Mongolia and yet it is even less impressive than Panj-kiang. There are only two mud houses and half a dozen *yurts* which seem to have been dropped carelessly behind a ragged hill.

After leaving Ude, we slipped rapidly up and down a succession of low hills and entered upon a plain so vast and flat that we appeared to be looking across an ocean. Not the smallest hill or rise of ground broke the line where earth and sky met in a faint blue haze. Our cars seemed like tiny boats in a limitless, grassy sea. It was sixty miles across, and for three hours the steady hum of the motor hardly ceased, for the road was smooth and hard. Halfway over we saw another great herd of antelope and several groups of ten or twelve. These were a different species from those we had killed, and I got a fine young buck. Twice wolves trotted across the plain, and at one, which was very inquisitive, I did some shooting which I vainly try to forget.

But most interesting to me among the wild life along our way was the bustard. It is a huge bird, weighing from fifteen to forty pounds, with flesh of such delicate flavor that it rivals our best turkey. I had always wanted to kill a bustard and my first one was neatly eviscerated at two hundred yards by a Savage bullet. I was more pleased than if I had shot an antelope, perhaps because it did much to revive my spirits after the episode of the wolf.

Sand grouse, beautiful little gray birds, with wings like pigeons and remarkable, padded feet, whistled over us as we rolled along the road, and my heart was sick with the thought of the excellent shooting we were missing. But there was no time to stop, except for such game as actually crossed our path, else we should never have arrived at Urga, the City of the Living God.

Speaking of gods, I must not forget to mention the great lamasery at Turin, about one hundred and seventy miles from Urga. For hours before we reached it we saw the ragged hills standing sharp and clear against the sky line. The peaks themselves are not more than two hundred feet in height, but they rise from a rocky plateau some distance above the level of the plain. It is a wild spot where some mighty internal force has burst the surface of the earth and pushed up a ragged core of rocks which have been carved by the knives of weather into weird, fantastic shapes. This elemental battle ground is a fit setting for the most remarkable group of human habitations that I have ever seen.

Three temples lie in a bowl-shaped hollow, surrounded by hundreds upon hundreds of tiny pill-box dwellings painted red and white. There must be a thousand of them and probably twice as many lamas. On the outskirts of the "city" to the south enormous piles of *argul* have been collected by the priests and bestowed as votive offerings by devout travelers. Vast as the supply seemed, it would take all this, and more, to warm the houses of the lamas during the bitter winter months when the ground is covered with snow. On the north the hills throw protecting arms about the homes of these half-wild men, who have chosen to spend their lives in this lonely desert stronghold. The houses are built of sawn boards, the first indication we had seen that we were nearing a forest country.

The remaining one hundred and seventy miles to Urga are a delight, even to the motorist who loves the paved roads of cities. They are like a boulevard amid glorious, rolling hills luxuriant with long, sweet grass. In the distance herds of horses and cattle grouped themselves into moving patches, and fat-tailed sheep dotted the plain like drifts of snow. I have seldom seen a better grazing country. It needed but little imagination to picture what it will be a few years hence when the inevitable railroad claims the desert as its own, for this rich land cannot long remain untenanted. It was here that we saw the first marmots, an unfailing indication that we were in a northern country.

The thick blackness of a rainy night had enveloped us

long before we swung into the Urga Valley and groped our way along the Tola River bank toward the glimmering lights of the sacred city. It seemed that we would never reach them, for twice we took the wrong turn and found ourselves in a maze of sandy bottoms and half-grown trees. But at ten o'clock we plowed through the mud of a narrow street and into the courtyard of the Mongolian Trading Company's home.

Oscar Mamen, Coltman's former partner, and Mrs. Mamen had spent several years there, and for six weeks they had had as guests Messrs. A. M. Guptil and E. B. Price, of Peking. Mr. Guptil was representing the American Military Attaché, and Mr. Price, Assistant Chinese Secretary of the American Legation, had come to Urga to establish communication with our consul at Irkutsk who had not been heard from for more than a month.

Urga recently had been pregnant with war possibilities. In the Lake Baikal region of Siberia there were several thousand Magyars and many Bolsheviki. It was known that Czechs expected to attack them, and that they would certainly be driven across the borders into Mongolia if defeated. In that event what would be the attitude of the Mongolian government? Would it intern the belligerents, or allow them to use the Urga district as a base of operations?

As a matter of fact, the question had been settled just before my arrival. The Czechs had made the expected attack with about five hundred men; all the Magyars, to the number of several thousand, had surrendered, and the Bolsheviki had disappeared like mists before the sun. The front of operations had moved in a single night almost two thousand miles away to the Omsk district, and it was certain that Mongolia would be left in peace. Mr. Price's work also was done, for the telegraph from Urga to Irkutsk was again in operation and thus communication was established with Peking.

The morning after my arrival Mr. Guptil and I rode out to see the town. Never have I visited such a city of contrasts, or one to which I was so eager to return. As we did come back, I shall tell, in a future chapter, of what we found there.

CHAPTER III
A CHAPTER OF ACCIDENTS

This is a "hard luck" chapter. Stories of ill-fortune are not always interesting, but I am writing this one to show what can happen to an automobile in the Gobi. We had gone to Urga without even a puncture and I began to feel that motoring in Mongolia was as simple as riding on Fifth Avenue—more so, in fact, for we did not have to watch traffic policemen or worry about "right of way." There is no crowding on the Gobi Desert. When we passed a camel caravan or a train of ox-carts we were sure to have plenty of room, for the landscape was usually spotted in every direction with fleeing animals.

Our motors had "purred" so steadily that accidents and repair shops seemed very far away and not of much importance. On the return trip, however, the reverse of the picture was presented and I learned that to be alone in the desert when something is wrong with the digestion of your automobile can have its serious aspects. Unless you are an expert mechanic and have an assortment of "spare parts," you may have to walk thirty or forty miles to the nearest water and spend many days of waiting until help arrives. Fortunately for us, there are few things which either Coltman or Guptil do not know about the "insides" of a motor and, moreover, after a diagnosis, they both have the ingenuity to remedy almost any trouble with a hammer and a screw driver.

Four days after our arrival in Urga we left on the return trip. As occupants of his car Charles Coltman had Mr. Price, Mrs. Coltman, and Mrs. Mamen. With the spiritual and physical assistance of Mr. Guptil I drove the second automobile, carrying in the rear seat a wounded Russian Cossack and a French-Czech, both couriers. The third car was a Ford *chassis* to which a wooden body had been affixed. It was designed to give increased carrying space, but it looked like a half-grown hayrack and was appropriately called the "agony box." This was driven by a chauffeur named Wang and carried Mamen's Chinese house boy and an *amah* besides a miscellaneous assortment of baggage.

It was a cold, gray morning when we started, with a cutting wind sweeping down from the north, giving a hint of the bitter winter which in another month would hold all Mongolia in an icy grasp. We made our way eastward up the valley to the Russian bridge across the Tola River and pointed the cars southward on the caravan trail to Kalgan.

Just as we reached the summit of the second long hill, across which the wind was sweeping in a glacial blast, there came a rasping crash somewhere in the motor of my car, followed by a steady *knock, knocks knock.* "That's a connecting rod as sure as fate," said "Gup." "We'll have to stop." When he had crawled under the car and found that his diagnosis was correct, he said a few other things which ought to have relieved his mind considerably.

There was nothing to be done except to replace the broken part with a spare rod. For three freezing hours Gup and Coltman lay upon their backs under the car, while the rest of us gave what help we could. To add to the difficulties a shower of hail swept down upon us with all the fury of a Mongolian storm. It was three o'clock in the afternoon before we were ready to go on, and our camp that night was only sixty miles from Urga.

The next day as we passed Turin the Czech pointed out the spot where he had lain for three days and nights with a broken collar bone and a dislocated shoulder. He had come from Irkutsk carrying important dispatches and had taken passage in an automobile belonging to a Chinese company which with difficulty was maintaining a passenger service between Urga and Kalgan. As usual, the native chauffeur was dashing along at thirty-five miles an hour when he should not have driven faster than twenty at the most. One of the front wheels slid into a deep rut, the car turned completely over and the resulting casualties numbered one man dead and our Czech seriously injured. It was three days before another car carried him back to Urga, where the broken bones were badly set by a drunken Russian doctor. The Cossack, too, had been shot twice in the heavy fighting on the Russian front, and, although his wounds were barely healed, he had just ridden three hundred miles on horseback with dispatches for Peking.

Both my passengers were delighted to have escaped the Chinese motors, for in them accidents had been the rule rather than the exception. During one year nineteen cars had been smashed and lay in masses of twisted metal beside the road. The difficulty had been largely due to the native chauffeurs. Although these men can drive a car, they have no mechanical training and danger signals from the motor are entirely disregarded. Moreover, all Chinese dearly love "show" and the chauffeurs delight in driving at tremendous speed over roads where they should exercise the greatest care. The deep cart ruts are a continual menace, for between them the road is often smooth and fine. But a stone or a tuft of grass may send one of the front wheels into a rut and capsize the car. Even with the greatest care accidents will happen, and motoring in Mongolia is by no means devoid of danger and excitement.

About three o'clock in the afternoon of the second day we saw frantic signals from the agony box which had been lumbering along behind us. It appeared that the right rear wheel was broken and the car could go no farther. There was nothing for it but to camp right where we were while Charles repaired the wheel. Gup and I ran twenty miles down the road to look for a well, but without success. The remaining water was divided equally among us but next morning we discovered that the Chinese had secreted two extra bottles for themselves, while we had been saving ours to the last drop. It taught me a lesson by which I profited the following summer.

On the third day the agony box limped along until noon, but when we reached a well in the midst of the great plain south of Turin it had to be abandoned, while we went on to Ude, the telegraph station in the middle of the desert, and wired Mamen to bring a spare wheel from Urga.

The fourth day there was more trouble with the connecting rod on my car and we sat for two hours at a well while the motor was eviscerated and reassembled. It had ceased to be a joke, especially to Coltman and Guptil, for all the work fell upon them. By this time they were almost unrecognizable because of dirt and grease and their hands were cut and blistered. But they stood it manfully, and at each new accident Gup rose to greater and greater heights of oratory.

We were halfway between Ude and Panj-kiang when we

saw two automobiles approaching from the south. Their occupants were foreigners we were sure, and as they stopped beside us a tall young man came up to my car. "I am Langdon Warner," he said. We shook hands and looked at each other curiously. Warner is an archæologist and Director of the Pennsylvania Museum. For ten years we had played a game of hide and seek through half the countries of the Orient and it seemed that we were destined never to meet each other. In 1910 I drifted into the quaint little town of Naha in the Loo-Choo Islands, that forgotten kingdom of the East. At that time it was far off the beaten track and very few foreigners had sought it out since 1854, when Commodore Perry negotiated a treaty with its king in the picturesque old Shuri Palace. Only a few months before I arrived, Langdon Warner had visited it on a collecting trip and the natives had not yet ceased to talk about the strange foreigner who gave them new baskets for old ones.

A little later Warner preceded me to Japan, and in 1912 I followed him to Korea. Our paths diverged when I went to Alaska in 1913, but I crossed his trail again in China, and in 1916, just before my wife and I left for Yün-nan, I missed him in Boston where I had gone to lecture at Harvard University. It was strange that after ten years we should meet for the first time in the middle of the Gobi Desert!

Warner was proceeding to Urga with two Czech officers who were on their way to Irkutsk. We gave them the latest news of the war situation and much to their disgust they realized that had they waited only two weeks longer they could have gone by train, for the attack by the Czechs on the Magyars and the Bolsheviki, in the trans-Baikal region, had cleared the Siberian railway westward as far as Omsk. After half an hour's talk we drove off in opposite directions. Warner eventually reached Irkutsk, but not without some interesting experiences with Bolsheviki along the way, and I did not see him again until last March (1920), when he came to my office in the American Museum just after we had returned to New York.

When we reached Panj-kiang we felt that our motor troubles were at an end, but ten miles beyond the station my car refused to pull through a sand pit and we found that there was trouble with the differential. It was necessary to dismantle the rear end of the car, and Coltman and Gup were well-nigh discouraged. The delay was a serious matter for I had urgent business in Japan, and it was imperative that I reach Peking as soon as possible. Charles finally decided to send me, together with Price, the Czech, and the Cossack, in his car, while he and Gup remained with the two ladies to repair mine.

Price and I drove back to Panj-kiang to obtain extra food and water for the working party and to telegraph Kalgan for assistance. We took only a little tea, macaroni, and two tins of sausage, for we expected to reach the mission station at Hei-ma-hou early the next morning.

We were hardly five miles from the broken car when we discovered that there was no more oil for our motor. It was impossible to go much farther and we decided that the only alternative was to wait until the relief party, for which we had wired, arrived from Kalgan. Just then the car swung over the summit of a rise, and we saw the white tent and grazing camels of an enormous caravan. Of course, Mongols would have mutton fat and why not use that for oil! The caravan leader assured us that he had fat in plenty and in ten minutes a great pot of it was warming over the fire.

We poured it into the motor and proceeded merrily on our way. But there was one serious obstacle to our enjoyment of that ride. Events had been moving so rapidly that we had eaten nothing since breakfast, and when a delicious odor of roast lamb began to arise from the motor, we realized that we were all very hungry. Dry macaroni would hardly do and the sausage must be saved for dinner. All the afternoon that tantalizing odor hovered in the air and I began to imagine that I could even smell mint sauce.

At six o'clock we saw the first *yurt* and purchased a supply of *argul* so that we could save time in making camp. The lamps of the car were *hors de combat* and a watery moon did not give us sufficient light by which to drive in safety, so we stopped on a hilltop shortly after dark. In the morning when the motor was cold we could save time and strength in cranking by pushing it down the slope.

PLATE III

The Middle Ages and the Twentieth Century

A Mongolian antelope killed from our motor cars

Watering camels at a well in the Gobi Desert

Much to our disgust we found that the *argul* we had purchased from the Mongol was so mixed with dirt that it would not burn. After half an hour of fruitless work I gave up, and we divided the tin of cold sausage. It was a pretty meager dinner for four hungry men and I retired into my sleeping bag to dream of roast lamb and mint sauce. When the Cossack officer found that he was not to have his tea he was like a child with a stick of candy just out of reach. He tried to sleep but it was no use, and in half an hour I opened my eyes to see him flat on his face blowing lustily at a piece of *argul* which he had persuaded to emit a faint glow. For two mortal hours the Russian nursed that fire until his pot of water reached the boiling point. Then he insisted that we all wake up to share his triumph.

We reached the mission station at noon next day, and Father Weinz, the Belgian priest in charge, gave us the first meal we had had in thirty-six hours. The Czech courier decided to remain at Hei-ma-hou and go in next day by cart, but we started immediately on the forty-mile horseback ride to Kalgan. A steady rain began about two o'clock in the afternoon, and in half an hour we were soaked to the skin; then the ugly, little gray stallion upon which I had been mounted planted both hind feet squarely on my left leg as we toiled up a long hill-trail to the pass, and I thought that my walking days had ended for all time. At the foot of the pass we halted at a dirty inn where they told us it would be useless to go on to Kalgan, for the gates of the city would certainly be closed and it would be impossible to enter until morning. There was no alternative except to spend the night at the inn, but as they had only a grass fire which burned out as soon as the cooking was finished, and as all our clothes were soaked, we spent sleepless hours shivering with cold.

The Cossack spoke only Mongol and Russian, and, as neither of us knew a single word of either language, it was difficult to communicate our plans to him. Finally, we found a Chinaman who spoke Mongol and who consented to act as interpreter. The natives at the inn could not understand why we were not able to talk to the Cossack. Didn't all white men speak the same language? Mr. Price endeavored to explain that Russian and English differ as much as do Chinese and

Mongol, but they only smiled and shook their heads.

In the morning I was so stiff from the kick which the gray stallion had given me that I could get to his back only with the greatest difficulty, but we reached Kalgan at eight o'clock. Unfortunately, the Cossack had left his passport in the cart which was to follow with his baggage, and the police at the gate would not let us pass. Mr. Price was well known to them and offered to assume responsibility for the Cossack in the name of the American Legation, but the policemen, who were much disgruntled at being roused so early in the morning, refused to let us enter.

Their attitude was so obviously absurd that we agreed to take matters into our own hands. We strolled outside the house and suddenly jumped on our horses. The sentries made a vain attempt to catch our bridle reins and we rode down the street at a sharp trot. There was another police station in the center of the city which it was impossible to avoid and as we approached it we saw a line of soldiers drawn up across the road. Our friends at the gate had telephoned ahead to have us stopped. Without hesitating we kept on, riding straight at the gray-clad policemen. With wildly waving arms they shouted at us to halt, but we paid not the slightest attention, and they had to jump aside to avoid being run down. The spectacle which these Chinese soldiers presented, as they tried to arrest us, was so ridiculous that we roared with laughter. Imagine what would happen on Fifth Avenue if you disregarded a traffic policeman's signal to stop!

Although the officials knew that we could be found at Mr. Coltman's house, we heard nothing further from the incident. It was so obviously a matter of personal ill nature on the part of the captain in charge of the gate police that they realized it was not a subject for further discussion.

After the luxury of a bath and shave we proceeded to Peking. Charles and Gup had rather a beastly time getting in. The car could not be repaired sufficiently to carry on under its own power, and, through a misunderstanding, the relief party only went as far as the pass and waited there for their arrival. They eventually found it necessary to hire three horses to tow them to the mission station where the "hard luck" story ended.

CHAPTER IV
NEW TRAVELS ON AN OLD TRAIL

The winter of 1918-19 we spent in and out of one of the most interesting cities in the world. Peking, with its background of history made vividly real by its splendid walls, its age-old temples and its mysterious Forbidden City, has a personality of its own.

When we had been away for a month or two there was always a delightful feeling of anticipation in returning to the city itself and to our friends in its cosmopolitan community.

Moreover, at our house in Wu Liang Tajen Hutung, a baby boy and his devoted nurse were waiting to receive us. Even at two years the extraordinary facility with which he discovered frogs and bugs, which, quite unknown to us, dwelt in the flower-filled courtyard, showed the hereditary instincts of a born explorer.

That winter gave us an opportunity to see much of ancient China, for we visited Shantung, traveled straight across the Provinces of Honan and Hupeh, and wandered about the mountains of Che-kiang on a serow hunt.

In February the equipment for our summer's work in Mongolia was on its way across the desert by caravan. We had sent flour, bacon, coffee, tea, sugar, butter and dried fruit, for these could be purchased in Urga only at prohibitive prices. Even then, with camel charges at fourteen cents a *cattie* ($1^1/_3$ lbs.), a fifty-pound sack of flour cost us more than six dollars by the time it reached Urga.

Charles Coltman at Kalgan very kindly relieved me of all the transportation details. We had seen him several times in Peking during the winter, and had planned the trip across the plains to Urga as *une belle excursion.*

Mrs. Coltman was going, of course, as were Mr. and Mrs. "Ted" MacCallie of Tientsin. "Mac" was a famous Cornell football star whom I knew by reputation in my own college days. He was to take a complete Delco electric lighting plant to Urga, with the hope of installing it in the palace of the "Living God."

A soldier named Owen from the Legation guard in Peking was to drive the Delco car, and I had two Chinese taxidermists, Chen and Kang, besides Lü, our cook and camp boy.

Chen had been loaned to me by Dr. J. G. Andersson, Mining Adviser to the Chinese Republic, and proved to be one of the best native collectors whom I have ever employed. The Coltmans and MacCallies were to stay only a few days in Urga, but they helped to make the trip across Mongolia one of the most delightful parts of our glorious summer.

We left Kalgan on May 17. Mac, Owen, and I rode the forty miles to Hei-ma-hou on horseback while Charles drove a motor occupied by the three women. There is a circuitous route by which cars can cross the pass under their own power, but Coltman preferred the direct road and sent four mules to tow the automobile up the mountains to the edge of the plateau.

It was the same trail I had followed the previous September. Then, as I stood on the summit of the pass gazing back across the far, dim hills, my heart was sad for I was about to enter a new land alone. My "best assistant" was on the ocean coming as fast as steam could carry her to join me in Peking. I wondered if Fate's decree would bring us here together that we might both have, as a precious heritage for future years, the memories of this strange land of romance and of mystery. Now the dream had been fulfilled and never have I entered a new country with greater hopes of what it would bring to me. Never, too, have such hopes been more gloriously realized.

We packed the cars that night and at half past five the next morning were on the road. The sky was gray and cloud-hung, but by ten o'clock the sun burned out and we gradually emerged from the fur robes in which we had been buried.

Instead of the fields of ripening grain which in the previous autumn had spread the hills with a flowing golden carpet, we saw blue-clad Chinese farmers turning long brown furrows with homemade plows. The trees about the mission station had just begun to show a tinge of green—the first sign of awakening at the touch of spring from the long winter sleep. Already caravans were astir, and we passed lines of laden camels now almost at the end of the long journey from Outer Mongolia, whither we were bound. But, instead of splendid beasts with upstanding humps and full neck beards, the camels now were pathetic mountains of almost naked skin on which the winter hair hung in ragged patches. The humps were loose and flat and flapped disconsolately as the great bodies lurched along the trail.

When we passed one caravan a *débonnaire* old Mongol wearing a derby hat swung out of line and signaled us to stop. After an appraising glance at the car he smiled broadly and indicated that he would like to race. In a moment he was off yelling at the top of his lungs and belaboring the bony sides of his camel with feet and hands. The animal's ungainly legs swung like a windmill in every direction it seemed, except forward, and yet the Mongol managed to keep his rolling old "ship of the desert" abreast of us for several minutes. Finally we let him win the race, and his look of delight was worth going far to see as he waved us good-by and with a hearty "*sai-bei-nah*" loped slowly back to the caravan.

The road was much better than it had been the previous fall. During the winter the constant tramp of padded feet had worn down and filled the ruts which had been cut by the summer traffic of spike-wheeled carts. But the camels had almost finished their winter's work. In a few weeks they would leave the trail to ox and pony caravans and spend the hot months in idleness, storing quantities of fat in their great hump reservoirs.

There was even more bird life than I had seen the previous September. The geese had all flown northward where we would find them scattered over their summer breeding grounds, but thousands of demoiselle cranes (*Anthropoides virgo*) had taken their places in the fields. They were in the midst of the spring courting and seemed to have lost all fear. One pair remained beside the road until we were less than twenty feet away, stepping daintily aside only when we threatened to run them down. Another splendid male performed a love dance for the benefit of his prospective bride quite undisturbed by the presence of our cars. With half-spread wings he whirled and leaped about the lady while every feather on her slim, blue body expressed infinite boredom and indifference to his passionate appeal.

Ruddy sheldrakes, mallards, shoveler ducks, and teal

were in even the smallest ponds and avocets with sky-blue legs and slender recurved bills ran along the shores of a lake at which we stopped for tiffin. When we had passed the last Chinese village and were well in the Mongolian grasslands we had great fun shooting gophers (*Citellus mongolicus umbratus*) from the cars. It was by no means easy to kill them before they slipped into their dens, and I often had to burrow like a terrier to pull them out even when they were almost dead.

We got eighteen, and camped at half past four in order that the taxidermists might have time to prepare the skins. There was a hint of rain in the air and we pitched the tent for emergencies, although none of us wished to sleep inside. Mac suggested that we utilize the electric light plant even if we were on the Mongolian plains. In half an hour he had installed wires in the tent and placed an arc lamp on the summit of a pole. It was an extraordinary experience to see the canvas walls about us, to hear the mournful wail of a lone wolf outside, and yet be able to turn the switch of an electric light as though we were in the city. No arc lamp on Fifth Avenue blazed more brightly than did this one on the edge of the Gobi Desert where none of its kind had ever shone before. With the motor cars which had stolen the sanctity of the plains it was only another evidence of the passing of Mongolian mystery.

Usually when we camped we could see, almost immediately, the silhouettes of approaching Mongols black against the evening sky. Where they came from we could never guess. For miles there might not have been the trace of a human being, but suddenly they would appear as though from out the earth itself. Perhaps they had been riding along some distant ridge far beyond the range of white men's eyes, or the roar of a motor had carried to their ears across the miles of plain; or perhaps it was that unknown sense, which seems to have been developed in these children of the desert, which directs them unerringly to water, to a lost horse, or to others of their kind. Be it what it may, almost every night the Mongols came loping into camp on their hardy, little ponies.

But this evening, when we had prepared an especial celebration, the audience did not arrive. It was a bitter disappointment, for we were consumed with curiosity to know what effect the blazing arc would have upon the Mongolian stoics. We could not believe that natives had not seen the light but probably they thought it was some spirit manifestation which was to be avoided. An hour after we were snuggled in our fur sleeping bags, two Mongols rode into camp, but we were too sleepy to give an exhibition of the fire-works.

We reached Panj-kiang about noon of the second day and found that a large mud house and a spacious compound had been erected beside the telegraph station by the Chinese company which was endeavoring to maintain a passenger service between Kalgan and Urga. The Chinese government also had invaded the field and was sending automobiles regularly to the Mongolian capital as a branch service of the Peking-Suiyuan railroad. In the previous September we had passed half a dozen of their motors in charge of a foreign representative of Messrs. Jardine, Matheson and Co. of Shanghai from whom the cars were purchased. He discovered immediately that the difficulties which the Chinese had encountered were largely the result of incompetent chauffeurs.

We had kept a sharp lookout for antelope, but saw nothing except a fox which looked so huge in the clear air that all of us were certain it was a wolf. There are always antelope on the Panj-kiang plain, however, and we loaded the magazines of our rifles as soon as we left the telegraph station. I was having a bit of sport with an immense flock of golden plover (*Pluvialis dominicus fulvus*) when the people in the cars signaled me to return, for a fine antelope buck was standing only a few hundred yards from the road. The ground was as smooth and hard as an asphalt pavement and we skimmed along at forty miles an hour. When the animal had definitely made up its mind to cross in front of us, Charles gave the accelerator a real push and the car jumped to a speed of forty-eight miles. The antelope was doing his level best to "cross our bows" but he was too far away, and for a few moments it seemed that we would surely crash into him if he held his course. It was a great race. Yvette had a death grip on my coat, for I was sitting half over the edge of the car ready to jump when Charles threw on the brakes. With any one but Coltman at the wheel I would have been too nervous to enjoy the ride, but we all had confidence in his superb driving.

PLATE IV

The water carrier for a caravan

A 35-pound buzzard

Young Mongolian

The buck crossed the road not forty yards in front of us, just at the summit of a tiny hill. Charles and I both fired once, and the antelope turned half over in a whirl of dust. It disappeared behind the hill crest and we expected to find it dead on the other side, but the slope was empty and even with our glasses we could not discover a sign of life on the plain, which stretched away to the horizon apparently as level as a floor. It had been swallowed utterly as though by the magic pocket of a conjurer.

Mac had not participated in the fun, for it had been a one-man race. Fifteen minutes later, however, we had a "free for all" which gave him his initiation.

An extract from Yvette's "Journal" gives her impression of the chase:

"Some one pointed out the distant, moving specks on the horizon and in a moment our car had left the road and started over the plains. Nearer and nearer we came, and faster and faster ran the antelope stringing out in a long, yellow line before us. The speedometer was moving up and up, thirty miles, thirty-five miles. Roy was sitting on the edge of the car with his legs hanging out, rifle in hand, ready to swing to the ground as soon as the car halted. Mr. Coltman, who was driving, had already thrown on the brakes, but Roy, thinking in his excitement that he had stopped, jumped—and jumped too soon. The speed at which we were going threw him violently to the ground. I hardly dared look to see what had happened but somehow he turned a complete somersault, landed on his knees, and instantly began shooting. Mr. Coltman, his hands trembling with the exertion of the drive, opened fire across the wind shield. As the first reports crashed out, the antelope, which had seemed to be flying before, flattened out and literally skimmed over the plain. Half a dozen bullets struck behind the herd, then as Roy's rifle cracked again, one of those tiny specks dropped to the ground.

"If was a wonderful shot—four hundred and twenty yards measured distance. No, this isn't a woman's inaccuracy of figures, it's a fact. But then you must remember the extraordinary clearness of the air in Mongolia, where every object appears to be magnified half a dozen times. The brilliant atmosphere is one of the most bewildering things of the desert. Once we thought we saw an antelope grazing on the hillside and Mr. Coltman remarked disdainfully: 'Pooh, that's a horse.' But the laugh was on him for as we drew near the 'horse' proved to be only a bleached bone. At a short distance camels and ponies stood out as though cut in steel, seeming as high as a village church steeple; and, most ridiculous of all, my husband mistook me once at a long, long distance for a telegraph pole! Tartarin de Tarascon would have had some wonderful stories to tell of Mongolia!"

We had hardly reached the road again before Mrs. Coltman discovered a great herd of antelope on the slope of a low hill, and when the cars carried us over the crest we could see animals in every direction, feeding in pairs or in groups of ten to forty.

We all agreed that no better place could be found at which to obtain motion pictures and camp was made forthwith. Unfortunately, the gazelles were shedding their winter coats and the skins were useless except for study; however, I did need half a dozen skeletons, so the animals we killed would not be wasted.

It was four o'clock in the afternoon when the tents were up and too late to take pictures; therefore, the photography was postponed until the next day, and we ran over toward a herd of antelope which was just visible on the sky line. When each of us had killed an animal, the opinion was unanimous that we had enough. I got mine on the first chase and thenceforth employed my time in making observations on the antelope's speed.

Time after time the car reached forty miles an hour, but with an even start the gazelles could swing about in front and "cross our bows." One of the antelope had a front leg broken just below the knee, and gave us a hard chase with the car going at thirty-five miles an hour. I estimated that even in its crippled condition the animal was traveling at a rate of *not less than twenty-five miles an hour.*

My field notes tell of a similar experience with the last gazelle which Mac killed late in the afternoon. "... We ran toward another group of antelope standing on the summit of a long land swell. There were fourteen in this herd and as the car neared them they trotted about with heads up, evidently trying to decide what species of plains animal we represented. The sun had just set, and I shall never forget the picture which they made, their graceful figures showing in black silhouettes against the rose glow of the evening sky. There was one buck among them and they seemed very nervous. When the men leaped out to shoot we were fully two hundred and fifty yards away, but at his third shot Mac dropped the buck. It was up again and off before the motor started in pursuit and, although running apart from the herd, it was only a short distance behind the others. Evidently the right foreleg was broken but with the car traveling at twenty-five miles an hour it was still drawing ahead. The going was not good and we ran for two miles without gaining an inch; then we came to a bit of smooth plain and the motor shot ahead at thirty-five miles an hour. We gained slowly and, when about one hundred yards away, I leaped out and fired at the animal breaking the other foreleg low down on the left side. Even with two legs injured it still traveled at a rate of fifteen miles, and a third shot was required to finish the unfortunate business. We found that both limbs were broken below the knee, and that the animal had been running on the stumps."

CHAPTER V
ANTELOPE MOVIE STARS

It was eight o'clock before we finished breakfast in the morning, but we did not wish to begin the motion picture photography until the sun was high enough above the horizon to give us a clear field for work. Charles and I rigged the tripod firmly in the *tonneau* of one of the cars. Mrs. Mac and Wang, a Chinese driver, were in the front seat, while Yvette and I squeezed in beside the camera. The Coltmans, Mac, and Owen occupied the other motor. We found a herd of antelope within a mile of camp and they, paraded in beautiful formation as the car approached. It would have made a splendid picture, but although the two automobiles were of the same make, there was a vast difference in their speed and it was soon evident that we could not keep pace with the other motor. After two or three ineffectual attempts we roped the camera in the most powerful car, the three men came in with me, and the women transferred to Wang's machine.

The last herd of antelope had disappeared over a long hill, and when we reached the summit we saw that they had separated into four groups and scattered about on the plains below us. We selected the largest, containing about fifty animals, and ran toward if as fast as the car could travel. The herd divided when we were still several hundred yards away, but the larger part gave promise of swinging across our path. The ground was thinly covered with short bunch grass, and when we reached a speed of thirty-five miles an hour the car was bounding and leaping over the tussocks like a ship in a heavy gale. I tried to stand, but after twice being almost pitched out bodily I gave it up and operated the camera by kneeling on the rear seat. Mac helped anchor me by sitting on my left leg, and we got one hundred feet of film from the first herd. Races with three other groups gave us two hundred feet more, and as the gasoline in our tank was alarmingly depleted we turned back toward camp.

Unfortunately I did not reload the camera with a fresh roll of film and thereby missed one of the most unusual and interesting pictures which ever could be obtained upon the plains. The tents were already in sight when a wolf suddenly appeared on the crest of a grassy knoll. He looked at us for a moment and then set off at an easy lope. The temptation was too great to be resisted even though there was a strong possibility that we might be stalled in the desert with no gas.

The ground was smooth and hard, and our speedometer showed forty miles an hour. We soon began to gain, but for three miles he gave us a splendid race. Suddenly, as we came over a low hill, we saw an enormous herd of antelope directly in front of us. They were not more than two hundred yards away, and the wolf made straight for them. Panic-stricken at the sight of their hereditary enemy followed by the roaring car, they scattered wildly and then swung about to cross our path. The wolf dashed into their midst and the herd divided as though cut by a knife. Some turned short about, but the others kept on toward us until I thought we would actually run them down. When not more than fifty yards from the motor they wheeled sharply and raced along beside the wolf.

To add to the excitement a fat, yellow marmot, which seemed suddenly to have lost his mind, galloped over the plain as fast as his short legs could carry him until he remembered that safety lay underground; then he popped into his burrow like a billiard ball into a pocket. With this strange assortment fleeing in front of the car we felt as though we had invaded a zoölogical garden.

The wolf paid not the slightest attention to the antelope for he had troubles of his own. We were almost on him, and I could see his red tongue between the foam-flecked jaws. Suddenly he dodged at right angles, and it was only by a clever bit of driving that Charles avoided crashing into him with the left front wheel. Before we could swing about the wolf had gained five hundred yards, but he was almost done. In another mile we had him right beside the car, and Coltman leaned far out to kill him with his pistol. The first bullet struck so close behind the animal that it turned him half over, and he dodged again just in time to meet a shot from Mac's rifle which broke his back. With its dripping lips drawn over a set of ugly teeth, the beast glared at us, as much as to say, "It is your move next, but don't come too close," Had it been any animal except a wolf I should have felt a twinge of pity, but I had no sympathy for the skulking brute. There will be more antelope next year because of its death.

All this had happened with an unloaded camera in the automobile. I had tried desperately to adjust a new roll of film, but had given up in despair for it was difficult enough even to sit in the bounding car. Were I to spend the remainder of my life in Mongolia there might never be such a chance again.

But we had an opportunity to learn just how fast a wolf can run, for the one we had killed was undoubtedly putting his best foot forward. I estimated that even at first he was not doing more than thirty-five miles an hour, and later we substantiated it on another, which gave us a race of twelve miles. With antelope which can reach fifty-five to sixty miles an hour a wolf has little chance, unless he catches them unawares, or finds the newly born young. To avoid just this the antelope are careful to stay well out on the plains where there are no rocks or hills to conceal a skulking wolf.

The wolf we had killed was shedding its hair and presented a most dilapidated, moth-eaten appearance; moreover, it had just been feeding on the carcass of a dead camel, which subsequently we discovered a mile away. When we reached camp I directed the two taxidermists to prepare the skeleton of the wolf, but to keep well away from the tents.

Charles and I had been talking a good deal about antelope steak, and for tiffin I had cut the fillets from one of the young gazelle. We were very anxious to "make good" on all that had been promised, so we cooked the steak ourselves. Just when the party was assembled in the tent for luncheon the Chinese began work upon the wolf. They had obediently gone to a considerable distance to perform the last rites, but had not chosen wisely in regard to the wind. As the antelope steak was brought in, a gentle breeze wafted with it a concentrated essence of defunct camel. Yvette put down her knife and fork and looked up. She caught my eye and burst out laughing. Mrs. Mac had her hand clasped firmly over her mouth and on her face was an expression of horror and deathly nausea.

Although I am a great lover of antelope steak, I will admit that when accompanied by *parfum de chameau*, especially when it is a very dead *chameau*, there are other things more attractive. Moreover, the antelope which we killed on the Panj-kiang plain really were very strong indeed. I have never been able to discover what was the cause, for those farther to the north were as delicious as any we have ever eaten. The introduction was such an unfortunate one that the party shied badly whenever antelope meat was mentioned during the remainder of the trip to Urga. Coltman, who had charge of the commissary, quite naturally expected that we would depend largely on meat and had not provided a sufficiency of other food. As a result we found that after the third day rations were becoming very short.

We camped that night at a well in a sandy river bottom about ten miles beyond Ude, the halfway point on the trip to Urga. It had been a bad day, with a bitterly cold wind which drove the dust and tiny pebbles against our faces like a continual storm of hail. As soon as the cars had stopped every one of us set to work with soap and water before anything had been done toward making camp. Our one desire was to remove a part of the dirt which had sifted into our eyes, hair, mouths, and ears. In half an hour we looked more brightly upon the world and began to wonder what we would have for dinner. It was a discussion which could not be carried on for very long since the bread was almost gone and only macaroni remained. Just then a demoiselle crane alighted beside the well not forty yards away. "There's our dinner," Charles shouted, "shoot it."

Two minutes later I was stripping off the feathers, and in less than five minutes it was sizzling in the pan. That was a bit too much for Mrs. Mac, hungry as she was. "Just think," she said, "that bird was walking about here not ten minutes ago and now it's on my plate. It hasn't stopped wiggling yet. I can't eat it!"

Poor girl, she went to bed hungry, and in the night waked to find her face terribly swollen from wind and sunburn. She was certain that she was about to die, but decided, like the "good sport" she is, to die alone upon the hillside where she wouldn't disturb the camp. After half an hour of wandering about she felt better, and returned to her sleeping bag on the sandy river bottom.

Just before dark we heard the *dong, dong, dong* of a

camel's bell and saw the long line of dusty yellow animals swing around a sharp earth-corner into the sandy space beside the well. Like the trained units of an army each camel came into position, kneeled upon the ground and remained quietly chewing its cud until the driver removed the load. Long before the last straggler had arrived the tents were up and a fire blazing, and far into the night the thirsty beasts grunted and roared as the trough was filled with water.

For thirty-six days they had been on the road, and yet were only halfway across the desert. Every day had been exactly like the day before—an endless routine of eating and sleeping, camp-making and camp-breaking in sun, rain, or wind. The monotony of it all would be appalling to a westerner, but the Oriental mind seems peculiarly adapted to accept it with entire contentment. Long before daylight they were on the road again, and when we awoke only the smoking embers of an *argul* fire remained as evidence that they ever had been there.

Mongolia, as we saw it in the spring, was very different from Mongolia of the early autumn. The hills and plains stretched away in limitless waves of brown untinged by the slightest trace of green, and in shaded corners among rocks there were still patches of snow or ice. Instead of resembling the grassy plains of Kansas or Nebraska, now it was like a real desert and I had difficulty in justifying to Yvette and Mac my glowing accounts of its potential resources.

Moreover, the human life was just as disappointing as the lack of vegetation, for we were "between seasons" on the trail. The winter traffic was almost ended, and the camels would not be replaced by cart caravans until the grass was long enough to provide adequate food for oxen and horses. The *yurts*, which often are erected far out upon the plains away from water when snow is on the ground, had all been moved near the wells or to the summer pastures; and sometimes we traveled a hundred miles without a glimpse of even a solitary Mongol.

Ude had been left far behind, and we were bowling along on a road as level as a floor, when we saw two wolves quietly watching us half a mile away. We had agreed not to chase antelope again; but wolves were fair game at any time.

Moreover, we were particularly glad to be able to check our records as to how fast a wolf can run when conditions are in its favor. Coltman signaled Mac to await us with the others, and we swung toward the animals which were trotting slowly westward, now and then stopping to look back as though reluctant to leave such an unusual exhibition as the car was giving them. A few moments later, however, they decided that curiosity might prove dangerous and began to run in earnest.

They separated almost immediately, and we raced after the larger of the two, a huge fellow with rangy legs which carried him forward in a long, swinging lope. The ground was perfect for the car, and the speedometer registered forty miles an hour. He had a thousand-yard start, but we gained rapidly, and I estimated that he never reached a greater speed than thirty miles an hour. Charles was very anxious to kill the brute from the motor with his .45 caliber automatic pistol, and I promised not to shoot.

The wolf was running low to the ground, his head a little to one side watching us with one bloodshot eye. He was giving us a great race, but the odds were all against him, and finally we had him right beside the motor. Leaning far out, Coltman fired quickly. The bullet struck just behind the brute, and he swerved sharply, missing the right front wheel by a scant six inches. Before Charles could turn the car he had gained three hundred yards, but we reached him again in little more than a mile. As Coltman was about to shoot a second time, the wolf suddenly dropped from sight. Almost on the instant the car plunged over a bank four feet in height, landed with a tremendous shock—and kept on! Charles had seen the danger in a flash, and had thrown his body against the wheel to hold it steady. Had he not been an expert driver we should inevitably have turned upside down and probably all would have been killed.

We stopped an instant to inspect the springs, but by a miracle not a leaf was broken. The wolf halted, too, and we could see him standing on a gentle rise with drooping head, his gray sides heaving. He seemed to be "all in," but to our amazement he was off again like the wind even before the car had started. During the last three miles the ground had been changing rapidly, and we soon reached a stony plain where there was imminent danger of smashing a front wheel. The wolf was heading directly toward a rocky slope which lay against the sky like the spiny back of some gigantic monster of the past.

His strategy had almost won the race. For a moment the wolf rested on the ridge, and I leaped out to shoot, but instantly he dropped behind the bowlders. Leaving me to intercept the animal, Charles swung behind the ridge only to run at full speed into a sandy pocket. The motor ceased to throb, and the race was ended.

These wolves are sneaking carrion-feeders and as such I detest them, but this one had "played the game." *For twelve long miles* he had kept doggedly at his work without a whimper or a cry of "kamerad." The brute had outgeneraled us completely, had won by strategy and magnificent endurance. Whatever he supposed the roaring car to be, instinct told him that safety lay among the rocks and he led us there as straight as an arrow's flight.

The animal seemed to take an almost human enjoyment in the way we had been tricked, for he stood on a hillside half a mile away watching our efforts to extricate the car. We were in a bad place, and it was evident that the only method of escape was to remove all the baggage which was tied to the running boards. Spreading our fur sleeping bags upon the sand, we pushed and lifted the automobile to firm ground after an hour of strenuous work. Hardly had we started back to the road, when Charles suddenly clapped both hands to his face yelling, "My Lord, I'm burning up. What is it? I'm all on fire."

Mrs. Coltman pulled his hands away, revealing his face covered with blotches and rising blisters. At the same moment Yvette and I felt a shower of liquid fire stinging our hands and necks. We leaped out of the car just as another blast swept back upon us. Then Charles shouted, "I know. It's the Delco plant," and dived toward the front mud guard. Sure enough, the cover had been displaced from one of the batteries, and little pools of sulphuric acid had formed on the leather casings. The wind was blowing half a gale, and each gust showered us with drops of colorless liquid which bit like tiny, living coals.

In less than ten seconds I had slashed the ropes and the batteries were lying on the ground, but the acid had already done its work most thoroughly. The duffle sacks containing all our field clothes had received a liberal dose, and during the summer Yvette was kept busy patching shirts and trousers. I never would have believed that a little acid could go so far. Even garments in the very center of the sacks would suddenly disintegrate when we put them on, and the Hutukhtu and his electric plant were "blessed" many times before we left Mongolia.

When we reached the road, Mrs. Mac was sitting disconsolately in a car beside the servants. We had been gone nearly three hours and the poor girl was frantic with anxiety. Mac and Owen had followed our tracks in another motor, and arrived thirty minutes later. Mac's happy face was drawn and white.

"I wouldn't go through that experience again for all the money in Mongolia," he said. "We followed your tracks and at every hill expected to find you dead on the other side and the car upside down. How on earth did you miss capsizing when you went over that bank?"

At Turin we found Mr. and Mrs. Mamen camped near the telegraph station awaiting our arrival. The first cry was "Food! Food!" and two loaves of Russian bread which they had brought from Urga vanished in less than fifteen minutes. After taking several hundred feet of "movie" film at the monastery, we ran on northward over a road which was as smooth and hard as a billiard table. The Turin plain was alive with game; marmots, antelope, hares, bustards, geese, and cranes seemed to have concentrated there as though in a vast zoölogical garden, and we had some splendid shooting. But as Yvette and I spent two glorious months on this same plain, I will tell in future chapters how, in long morning horseback rides and during silent starlit nights, we learned to know and love it.

PLATE V

Mongol horsemen on the streets of Urga

The prison at Urga

A criminal in a coffin with hands manacled

CHAPTER VI
THE SACRED CITY OF THE LIVING BUDDHA

Far up in northern Mongolia, where the forests stretch in an unbroken line to the Siberian frontier, lies Urga, the Sacred City of the Living Buddha. The world has other sacred cities, but none like this. It is a relic of medieval times overlaid with a veneer of twentieth-century civilization; a city of violent contrasts and glaring anachronisms. Motor cars pass camel caravans fresh from the vast, lone spaces of the Gobi Desert; holy lamas, in robes of flaming red or brilliant yellow, walk side by side with black-gowned priests; and swarthy Mongol women, in the fantastic headdress of their race, stare wonderingly at the latest fashions of their Russian sisters.

We came to Urga from the south. All day we had been riding over rolling, treeless uplands, and late in the afternoon we had halted on the summit of a hill overlooking the Tola River valley. Fifteen miles away lay Urga, asleep in the darkening shadow of the Bogdo-ol (God's Mountain). An hour later the road led us to our first surprise in Mai-ma-cheng, the Chinese quarter of the city. Years of wandering in the strange corners of the world had left us totally unprepared for what we saw. It seemed that here in Mongolia we had discovered an American frontier outpost of the Indian fighting days. Every house and shop was protected by high stockades of unpeeled timbers, and there was hardly a trace of Oriental architecture save where a temple roof gleamed above the palisades.

Before we were able to adjust our mental perspective we had passed from colonial America into a hamlet of modern Russia. Gayly painted cottages lined the road, and, unconsciously, I looked for a white church with gilded cupolas. The church was not in sight, but its place was taken by a huge red building of surpassing ugliness, the Russian Consulate. It stands alone on the summit of a knoll, the open plains stretching away behind it to the somber masses of the northern forests. In its imposing proportions it is tangible evidence of the Russian Colossus which not many years ago dominated Urga and all that is left of the ancient empire of the Khans.

For two miles the road is bordered by Russian cottages; then it debouches into a wide square which loses its distinctive character and becomes an indescribable mixture of Russia, Mongolia, and China. Palisaded compounds, gay with fluttering prayer flags, ornate houses, felt-covered *yurts*, and Chinese shops mingle in a dizzying chaos of conflicting personalities. Three great races have met in Urga and each carries on, in this far corner of Mongolia, its own customs and way of life. The Mongol *yurt* has remained unchanged; the Chinese shop, with its wooden counter and blue-gowned inmates, is pure Chinese; and the ornate cottages proclaim themselves to be only Russian.

But on the street my wife and I could never forget that we were in Mongolia. We never tired of wandering through the narrow alleys, with their tiny native shops, or of watching the ever-changing crowds. Mongols in half a dozen different tribal dresses, Tibetan pilgrims, Manchu Tartars, or camel drivers from far Turkestan drank and ate and gambled with Chinese from civilized Peking.

The barbaric splendor of the native dress fairly makes one gasp for breath. Besides gowns and sashes of dazzling brilliance, the men wear on their heads all the types of covering one learned to know in the pictures of ancient Cathay, from the high-peaked hat of yellow and black—through the whole, strange gamut—to the helmet with streaming peacock plumes. But were I to tell about them all I would leave none of my poor descriptive phrases for the women.

It is hopeless to draw a word-picture of a Mongol woman. A photograph will help, but to be appreciated she must be seen in all her colors. To begin with the dressing of her hair. If all the women of the Orient competed to produce a strange and fantastic type, I do not believe that they could excel what the Mongol matrons have developed by themselves.

Their hair is plaited over a frame into two enormous flat bands, curved like the horns of a mountain sheep and reënforced with bars of wood or silver. Each horn ends in a silver plaque, studded with bits of colored glass or stone, and supports a pendent braid like a riding quirt. On her head, between the horns, she wears a silver cap elaborately chased and flashing with "jewels." Surmounting this is a "saucer" hat of black and yellow. Her skirt is of gorgeous brocade or cloth, and the jacket is of like material with prominent "puffs" upon the shoulders. She wears huge leather boots with upturned, pointed toes, similar to those of the men, and when in full array she has a whole portière of beadwork suspended from the region of her ears.

She is altogether satisfying to the lover of fantastic Oriental costumes, except in the matter of footgear, and this slight exception might be allowed, for she has so amply decorated every other available part of her anatomy.

Moreover, the boots form a very necessary adjunct to her personal equipment, besides providing a covering for her feet. They are many sizes too large, of course, but they furnish ample space during the bitter cold of winter for the addition of several pairs of socks, varying in number according to the thermometer. During the summer she often wears no socks at all, but their place is taken by an assortment of small articles which cannot be carried conveniently on her person. Her pipe and tobacco, a package of tea, or a wooden bowl can easily be stuffed into the wide top boots, for pockets are an unknown luxury even to the men.

In its kaleidoscopic mass of life and color the city is like a great pageant on the stage of a theater, with the added fascination of reality. But, somehow, I could never quite make myself believe that it was real when a brilliant group of horsemen in pointed, yellow hats and streaming, peacock feathers dashed down the street. It seemed too impossible that I, a wandering naturalist of the drab, prosaic twentieth century, and my American wife were really a living, breathing part of this strange drama of the Orient.

But there was one point of contact which we had with this dream-life of the Middle Ages. Yvette and I both love horses, and the way to a Mongol's heart is through his pony. Once on horseback we began to identify ourselves with the fascinating life around us. We lost the uncomfortable sense of being merely spectators in the Urga theatricals, and forgot that we had come to the holy city by means of a very unromantic motor car.

We remained at Urga for ten days while preparations were

under way for our first trip to the plains, and returned to it often during the summer. We came to know it well, and each time we rode down the long street it seemed more wonderful that, in these days of commerce, Urga, and in fact all Mongolia, could have existed throughout the centuries with so little change.

There is, of course, no lack of modern influence in the sacred city, but as yet it is merely a veneer which has been lightly superimposed upon its ancient civilization, leaving almost untouched the basic customs of its people. This has been due to the remoteness of Mongolia. Until a few years ago, when motor cars first made their way across the seven hundred miles of plains, the only access from the south was by camel caravan, and the monotonous trip offered little inducement to casual travelers. The Russians came to Urga from the north and, until the recent war, their influence was paramount along the border. They were by no means anxious to have other foreigners exploit Mongolia, and they wished especially to keep the country as a buffer-state between themselves and China.

Not only is Urga the capital of Mongolia and the only city of considerable size in the entire country but it is also the residence of the Hutukhtu, or Living Buddha, the head of both the Church and the State. Across the valley his palaces nestle close against the base of the Bogdo-ol (God's Mountain), which rises in wooded slopes from the river to an elevation of eleven thousand feet above sea level.

The Sacred Mountain is a vast game preserve, which is patrolled by two thousand lamas, and every approach is guarded by a temple or a camp of priests. Great herds of elk, roebuck, boar, and other animals roam the forests, but to shoot within the sacred precincts would mean almost certain death for the transgressor. Some years ago several Russians from Urga made their way up the mountain during the night and killed a bear. They were brought back in chains by a mob of frenzied lamas. Although the hunters had been beaten nearly to death, it required all the influence of the Russian diplomatic agent to save what remained of their lives.

The Bogdo-ol extends for twenty-five miles along the Tola Valley, shutting off Urga from the rolling plains to the south. Like a gigantic guardian of the holy city at its base, it stands as the only obstacle to the wireless station which is soon to be erected.

The Hutukhtu has three palaces on the banks of the Tola River. One of them is a hideous thing, built in Russian style. The other two at least have the virtue of native architecture. In the main palace the central structure is white with gilded cupolas, and smaller pavilions at the side have roofs of green. The whole is surrounded by an eight-foot stockade of white posts trimmed with red.

The Hutukhtu seldom leaves his palace now, for he is old and sick and almost blind. Many strange stories are told of the mysterious "Living God" which tend to show him "as of the earth earthy." It is said that in former days he sometimes left his "heaven" to revel with convivial foreigners in Urga; but all this is gossip and we are discussing a very saintly person. His passion for Occidental trinkets and inventions is well known, however, and his palace is a veritable storehouse for gramophones, typewriters, microscopes, sewing machines, and a host of other things sold to him by Russian traders and illustrated in picture catalogues sent from the uttermost corners of the world. But like a child he soon tires of his toys and throws them aside. He has a motor car, but he never rides in it. It has been reported that his chief use for the automobile is to attach a wire to its batteries and give his ministers an electric shock; for all Mongols love a practical joke, and the Hutukhtu is no exception.

Now his palace is wired for electricity, and a great arc light illuminates the courtyard. One evening Mr. Lucander and Mr. Mamen, who sold the electric plant to the Hutukhtu, were summoned to the palace to receive payment. They witnessed a scene which to-day could be possible only in Mongolia. Several thousand dollars in silver were brought outside to their motor car, and the lama, who paid the bills, insisted that they count it in his presence.

A great crowd of Mongols had gathered near the palace and at last a long rope was let out from one of the buildings. Kneeling, the Mongols reverently touched the rope, which was gently waggled from the other end, supposedly by the Hutukhtu. A barbaric monotone of chanted prayers arose from the kneeling suppliants, and the rope was waggled again. Then the Mongols rode away, silent with awe at having been blessed by the Living God. All this under a blazing electric light beside an automobile at the foot of the Bogdo-ol!

The Hutukhtu seemed to feel that it became his station as a ruling monarch to have a foreign house with foreign furniture. Of course he never intended to live in it, but other kings had useless palaces and why shouldn't he? Therefore, a Russian atrocity of red brick was erected a half mile or so from his other dwellings. The furnishing became a matter of moment, and Mr. Lucander, who was temporarily in the employ of the Mongolian Government, was intrusted with the task of attending to the intimate details. The selection of a bed was most important, for even Living Buddhas have to sleep sometimes—they cannot always be blessing adoring subjects or playing jokes on their ministers of state. With considerable difficulty a foreign bed was purchased and brought across the seven hundred miles of plains and desert to the red brick palace on the banks of the Tola River.

Mr. Lucander superintended its installation in the Hutukhtu's boudoir and himself turned chambermaid. As this was the first time he had ever made a bed for a Living God, he arranged the spotless sheets and turned down the covers with the greatest care. When all was done to his satisfaction he reported to one of the Hutukhtu's ministers that the bed was ready. Two lamas, high dignitaries of the church, were the inspection committee. They agreed that it *looked* all right, but the question was, how did it *feel?* Mr. Lucander waxed eloquent on the "springiness" of the springs, and assured them that no bed could be better; that this was the bed *par excellence* of all the beds in China. The lamas held a guttural consultation and then announced that before the bed could be accepted it must be tested. Therefore, without more ado, each lama in his dirty boots and gown laid his unwashed self upon the bed, and bounced up and down. The result was satisfactory—except to Lucander and the sheets.

Although to foreign eyes and in the cold light of modernity the Hutukhtu and his government cut a somewhat ridiculous figure, the reverse of the picture is the pathetic death struggle of a once glorious race. I have said that unaccustomed luxury was responsible for the decline of the Mongol Empire, but the ruin of the race was due to the Lama Church. Lamaism, which was introduced from Tibet, gained its hold not long after the time of Kublai Khan's death in 1295. Previous to this the Mongols had been religious liberals, but eventually Lamaism was made the religion of the state. It is a branch of the Buddhist cult, and its teachings are against war and violent death.

By custom one or more sons of every family are dedicated to the priesthood, and as Lamaism requires its priests to be celibate, the birth rate is low. To-day there are only a few million Mongols in a country half as large as the United States (exclusive of Alaska), a great proportion of the male population being lamas. With no education, except in the books of their sect, they lead a lazy, worthless existence, supported by the lay population and by the money they extract by preying upon the superstitions of their childlike brothers. Were Lamaism abolished there still would be hope for Mongolia under a proper government, for the Mongols of to-day are probably the equals of Genghis Khan's warriors in strength, endurance, and virility.

The religion of Mongolia is like that of Tibet and the Dalai Lama of Lhassa is the head of the entire Church. The Tashi Lama residing at Tashilumpo, also in Tibet, ranks second. The Hutukhtu of Mongolia is third in the Lama hierarchy, bearing the title *Cheptsundampa Hutukhtu* (Venerable Best Saint). According to ancient tradition, the Hutukhtu never dies; his spirit simply reappears in the person of some newly born infant and thus comes forth reëmbodied. The names of infants, who have been selected as possible candidates for the honor, are written upon slips of paper incased in rolls of paste and deposited in a golden urn. The one which is drawn is hailed as the new incarnation.

Some years ago the eyesight of the Hutukhtu began to fail, and a great temple was erected as a sacrifice to appease the gods. It stands on a hill at the western end of Urga, surrounded by the tiny wooden dwellings of the priests. "The Lama City" it is called, for only those in the service of the Church are allowed to live within its sacred precincts. In the temple itself there is an eighty-foot bronze image of Buddha standing on a golden lotus flower. The great figure is heavily gilded, incrusted with precious stones, and draped with silken cloths.

I was fortunate in being present one day when the temple was opened to women and the faithful in the city. Somewhat doubtful as to my reception, I followed the crowd as it filed through an outer pavilion between a double row of kneeling lamas in high-peaked hats and robes of flaming yellow. I carried my hat in my hand and tried to wear a becoming expression of humility and reverence. It was evidently successful, for I passed unhindered into the Presence. At the entrance stood a priest who gave me, with the others, a few drops of holy water from a filthy jug. Silent with awe, the people bathed their faces with the precious fluid and prostrated themselves before the gigantic figure standing on the golden lotus blossom, its head lost in the shadows of the temple roof. They kissed its silken draperies, soiled by the lips of other thousands, and each one gathered a handful of sacred dirt from the temple floor. From niches in the walls hundreds of tiny Buddhas gazed impassively on the worshiping Mongols.

The scene was intoxicating in its barbaric splendor. The women in their fantastic headdresses and brilliant gowns; the blazing yellow robes of the kneeling lamas; and the chorus of prayers which rose and fell in a meaningless half-wild chant broken by the clash of cymbals and the boom of drums—all this set the blood leaping in my veins. There was a strange dizziness in my head, and I had an almost overpowering desire to fall on my knees with the Mongols and join in the chorus of adoration. The subtle smell of burning incense, the brilliant colors, and the barbaric music were like an intoxicating drink which inflamed the senses but dulled the brain. It was then that I came nearest to understanding the religious fanaticism of the East. Even with a background of twentieth-century civilization I felt its sensuous power. What wonder that it has such a hold on a simple, uneducated people, fed on superstition from earliest childhood and the religious traditions of seven hundred years!

PLATE VI

*The Great Temple
at Urga*

*A prayer wheel and a Mongol
lama*

Lamas calling the gods at a temple in Urga

Mongol praying at a shrine in Urga

The service ended abruptly in a roar of sound. Rising to their feet, the people streamed into the courtyard to whirl the prayer wheels about the temple's base. Each wheel is a hollow cylinder of varying size, standing on end, and embellished with Tibetan characters in gold. The wheels are sometimes filled with thousands of slips of paper upon which is written a prayer or a sacred thought, and each revolution adds to the store of merit in the future life.

The Mongol goes farther still in accumulating virtue, and every native house in Urga is gay with fluttering bits of cloth or paper on which a prayer is written. Each time the little flag moves in the wind it sends forth a supplication for the welfare of the Mongol's spirit in the Buddhistic heaven. Not only are the prayer wheels found about the temples, but they line the streets, and no visiting Mongol need be deprived of trying the virtue of a new device without going to a place of worship. He can give a whirl or two to half a dozen within a hundred yards of where he buys his tea or sells his sheep.

On every hand there is constant evidence that Urga is a sacred city. It never can be forgotten even for a moment. The golden roofs of scores of temples give back the sunlight, and the moaning chant of praying lamas is always in the air. Even in the main street I have seen the prostrate forms of ragged pilgrims who have journeyed far to this Mecca of the lama faith. If they are entering the city for the first time and crave exceeding virtue, they approach the great temple on the hill by lying face down at every step and beating their foreheads upon the ground. Wooden shrines of dazzling whiteness stand in quiet streets or cluster by themselves behind the temples. In front of each, raised slightly at one end, is a prayer board worn, black and smooth by the prostrated bodies of worshiping Mongols.

Although the natives take such care for the repose of the spirit in after life, they have a strong distaste for the body from which the spirit has fled and they consider it a most undesirable thing to have about the house. The stigma is imposed even upon the dying. In Urga a family of Mongols had erected their *yurt* in the courtyard of one of our friends. During the summer the young wife became very ill, and when her husband was convinced that she was about to die he moved the poor creature bodily out of the *yurt*. She could die if she wished, but it must not be inside his house.

The corpse itself is considered unclean and the abode of evil spirits, and as such must be disposed of as quickly as possible. Sometimes the whole family will pack up their *yurt* and decamp at once, leaving the body where it lies. More usually the corpse is loaded upon a cart which is driven at high speed over a bit of rough ground. The body drops off at some time during the journey, but the driver does not dare look back until he is sure that the unwelcome burden is no longer with him; otherwise he might anger the spirit following the corpse and thereby cause himself and his family unending trouble. Unlike the Chinese, who treat their dead with the greatest respect and go to enormous expense in the burial, every Mongol knows that his coffin will be the stomachs of dogs, wolves, or birds. Indeed, the Chinese name for the raven is the "Mongol's coffin."

The first day we camped in Urga, my wife and Mrs. MacCallie were walking beside the river. Only a short distance from our tent they discovered a dead Mongol who had just been dragged out of the city. A pack of dogs were in the midst of their feast and the sight was most unpleasant.

The dogs of Mongolia are savage almost beyond belief. They are huge black fellows like the Tibetan mastiff, and their diet of dead human flesh seems to have given them a contempt for living men. Every Mongol family has one or more, and it is exceedingly dangerous for a man to approach a *yurt* or caravan unless he is on horseback or has a pistol ready. In Urga itself you will probably be attacked if you walk unarmed through the meat market at night. I have never visited Constantinople, but if the Turkish city can boast of more dogs than Urga, it must be an exceedingly disagreeable place in which to dwell. Although the dogs live to a large extent upon human remains, they are also fed by the lamas. Every day about four o'clock in the afternoon you can see a cart being driven through the main street, followed by scores of yelping dogs. On it are two or more dirty lamas with a great barrel from which they ladle out refuse for the dogs, for according to their religious beliefs they accumulate great merit for themselves if they prolong the life of anything, be it bird, beast, or insect.

In the river valley, just below the Lama City, numbers of dogs can always be found, for the dead priests usually are thrown there to be devoured. Dozens of white skulls lie about in the grass, but it is a serious matter even to touch one. I very nearly got into trouble one day by targeting my rifle upon a skull which lay two or three hundred yards away from our tent.

The customs of the Mongols are not all as gruesome as those I have described, yet Urga is essentially a frontier city where life is seen in the raw. Its natives are a hard-living race, virile beyond compare. Children of the plains, they are accustomed to privation and fatigue. Their law is the law of the northland:

".... That only the Strong shall thrive,

That surely the Weak shall perish and only the Fit survive."

In the careless freedom of his magnificent horsemanship a Mongol seems as much an untamed creature of the plains as does the eagle itself which soars above his *yurt*. Independence breathes in every movement; even in his rough good humor and in the barbaric splendor of the native dress.

But the little matter of cleanliness is of no importance in his scheme of life. When a meal has been eaten, the wooden bowl is licked clean with the tongue; it is seldom washed. Every man and woman usually carries through life the bodily dirt which has accumulated in childhood, unless it is removed by some accident or by the wear of years. One can be morally certain that it will never be washed off by design or water. Perhaps the native is not altogether to blame, for, except in the north, water is not abundant. It can be found on the plains and in the Gobi Desert only at wells and an occasional pond, and on the march it is too precious to be wasted in the useless process of bathing. Moreover, from September until May the bitter winds which sweep down from the Siberian steppes furnish an unpleasant temperature in which to take a bath.

The Mongol's food consists almost entirely of mutton, cheese, and tea. Like all northern people, he needs an abundance of fat, and sheep supply his wants. There is always more or less grease distributed about his clothes and person, and when Mongols are *en masse* the odor of mutton and unwashed humanity is well-nigh overpowering.

I must admit that in morality the Mongol is but little better off than in personal cleanliness. A man may have only one lawful wife, but may keep as many concubines as his means allow, all of whom live with the members of the family in the single room of the *yurt*. Adultery is openly practiced, apparently without prejudice to either party, and polyandry is not unusual in the more remote parts of the country.

The Mongol is *unmoral* rather than immoral. He lives like an untaught child of nature and the sense of modesty or decency, as we conceive it, does not enter into his scheme of life. But the operation of natural laws, which in the lower animals are successful in maintaining the species, is fatally impaired by the loose family relations which tend to spread disease. Unless Lamaism is abolished I can see little hope for the rejuvenation of the race.

In writing of Urga's inhabitants and their way of life I am neglecting the city itself. I have already told of the great temple on the hill and its clustering lama houses which overlook and dominate the river valley. Its ornate roof, flashing in the sun, can be seen for many miles, like a religious beacon guiding the steps of wandering pilgrims to the Mecca of their faith.

At the near end of the broad street below the Lama City is the tent market, and just beyond it are the black-smith shops where bridles, cooking pots, tent pegs, and all the equipment essential to a wandering life on the desert can be purchased in an hour—if you have the price! Nothing is cheap in Urga, with the exception of horses, and when we began to outfit for our trip on the plains we received a shock similar to that which I had a month ago in New York, when I paid twenty dollars for a pair of shoes. We ought to be hardened to it now, but when we were being robbed in Urga by profiteering Chinese, who sell flour at ten and twelve dollars a sack and condensed milk at seventy-five cents a tin, we roared and grumbled—and paid the price! I vowed I would never pay twenty dollars for a pair of shoes at home, but roaring and grumbling is no more effective in procuring shoes in New York than it was in obtaining flour and milk in Urga.

We paid in Russian rubles, then worth three cents each. (In former years a ruble equaled more than half a dollar.) Eggs were well-nigh nonexistent, except those which had made their way up from China over the long caravan trail and were guaranteed to be "addled"—or whatever it is that sometimes makes an egg an unpleasant companion at the breakfast table. Even those cost three rubles each! Only a few Russians own chickens in Urga and their productions are well-nigh "golden eggs," for grain is very scarce and it takes an astounding number of rubles to buy a bushel.

Fortunately we had sent most of our supplies and equipment to Urga by caravan during the winter, but there were a good many odds and ends needed to fill our last requirements, and we came to know the ins and outs of the sacred city intimately before we were ready to leave for the plains. The Chinese shops were our real help, for in Urga, as everywhere else in the Orient, the Chinese are the most successful merchants. Some firms have accumulated considerable wealth and the Chinaman does not hesitate to exact the last cent of profit when trading with the Mongols.

At the eastern end of Urga's central street, which is made picturesque by gayly painted prayer wheels and alive with a moving throng of brilliant horsemen, are the Custom House and the Ministry of Foreign Affairs. The former is at the far end of an enormous compound filled with camel caravans or loaded carts. There is a more or less useless wooden building, but the business is conducted in a large *yurt*, hard against the compound wall. It was an extraordinary contrast to see a modern filing-cabinet at one end and a telephone box on the felt-covered framework of the *yurt*.

Not far beyond the Custom House is what I believe to be one of the most horrible prisons in the world. Inside a double palisade of unpeeled timbers is a space about ten feet square upon which open the doors of small rooms, almost dark. In these dungeons are piled wooden boxes, four feet long by two and one-half feet high. These coffins are the prisoners' cells.

Some of the poor wretches have heavy chains about their necks and both hands manacled together. They can neither sit erect nor lie at full length. Their food, when the jailer remembers to give them any, is pushed through a six-inch hole in the coffin's side. Some are imprisoned here for only a few days or weeks; others for life, or for many years. Sometimes they lose the use of their limbs, which shrink and shrivel away. The agony of their cramped position is beyond the power of words to describe. Even in winter, when the temperature drops, as it sometimes does, to sixty degrees below zero, they are given only a single sheepskin for covering. How it is possible to live in indescribable filth, half-fed, well-nigh frozen in winter, and suffering the tortures of the damned, is beyond my ken—only a Mongol could live at all.

The prison is not a Mongol invention. It was built by the Manchus and is an eloquent tribute to a knowledge of the fine arts of cruelty that has never been surpassed.

I have given this description of the prison not to feed morbid curiosity, but to show that Urga, even if it has a Custom House, a Ministry of Foreign Affairs, motor cars, and telephones, is still at heart a city of the Middle Ages.

In Urga we made a delightful and most valuable friend in the person of Mr. F. A. Larsen. Most foreigners speak of him as "Larsen of Mongolia" and indeed it is difficult for us to think of the country without thinking of the man. Some thirty years ago he rode into Mongolia and liked it. He liked it so much, in fact, that he dug a well and built a house among the Tabool hills a hundred miles north of Kalgan. At first he labored with his wife as a missionary, but later he left that field to her and took up the work which he loved best in all the world—the buying and selling of horses.

During his years of residence in Mongolia hundreds of thousands of horses have passed under his appraising eyes and the Mongols respect his judgment as they respect the man. I wish that I might write the story of his life, for it is more interesting than any novel of romance or adventure. In almost every recent event of importance to the Mongols Mr. Larsen's name has figured. Time after time he has been sent as an emissary of the Living Buddha to Peking when misunderstandings or disturbances threatened the political peace of Mongolia. Not only does he understand the psychology of the natives, but he knows every hill and plain of their vast plateau as well as do the desert nomads.

PLATE VII

*Mongol women beside a
"yurt"*

*The headdress of a Mongol
married woman*

The framework of a yurt

Mongol women and a lama

For some time he had been in charge of Andersen, Meyer's branch at Urga with Mr. E. W. Olufsen and we made their house our headquarters. Mr. Larsen immediately undertook to obtain an outfit for our work upon the plains. He purchased two riding ponies for us from Prince Tze Tze; he borrowed two carts with harness from a Russian friend, and bought another; he loaned us a riding pony for our Mongol, a cart horse of his own, and Mr. Olufsen contributed another. He made our equipment a personal matter and he was never too busy to assist us in the smallest details. Moreover, we could spend hours listening to the tales of his early life, for his keen sense of humor made him a delightful story-teller. One of the most charming aspects of our wandering life is the friends we have made in far corners of the world, and for none have we a more affectionate regard than for "Larsen of Mongolia."

CHAPTER VII
THE LONG TRAIL TO SAIN NOIN KHAN

Our arrival in Urga was in the most approved manner of the twentieth century. We came in motor cars with much odor of gasoline and noise of horns. When we left the sacred city we dropped back seven hundred years and went as the Mongols traveled. Perhaps it was not quite as in the days of Genghis Khan, for we had three high-wheeled carts of a Russian model, but they were every bit as springless and uncomfortable as the palanquins of the ancient emperors.

Of course, we ourselves did not ride in carts. They were driven by our cook and the two Chinese taxidermists, each of whom sat on his own particular mound of baggage with an air of resignation and despondency. Their faces were very long indeed, for the sudden transition from the back seat of a motor car to a jolting cart did not harmonize with their preconceived scheme of Mongolian life. But they endured it manfully, and doubtless it added much to the store of harrowing experience with which they could regale future audiences in civilized Peking.

My wife and I were each mounted on a Mongol pony. Mine was called "Kublai Khan" and he deserved the name. Later I shall have much to tell of this wonderful horse, for I learned to love him as one loves a friend who has endured the "ordeal by fire" and has not been found wanting. My wife's chestnut stallion was a trifle smaller than Kublai Khan and proved to be a tricky beast whom I could have shot with pleasure. To this day she carries the marks of both his teeth and hoofs, and we have no interest in his future life. Kublai Khan has received the reward of a sunlit stable in Peking where carrots are in abundance and sugar is not unknown.

Besides the three Chinese we had a little Mongol priest, a yellow lama only eighteen years of age. We did not hire him for spiritual reasons, but to be our guide and social mentor upon the plains. Of course, we could not speak Mongol, but both my wife and I know some Chinese and our cook-boy Lü was possessed of a species of "pidgin English" which, by using a good deal of imagination, we could understand at times. Since our lama spoke fluent Chinese, he acted as interpreter with the Mongols, and we had no difficulty. It is wonderful how much you can do with sign language when you really have to, especially if the other fellow tries to understand. You always can be sure that the Mongols will match your efforts in this respect.

An interesting part of our equipment was a Mongol tent which Charles Coltman had had made for us in Kalgan. This is an ingenious adaptation of the ordinary wall tent, and is especially fitted for work on the plains. No one should attempt to use any other kind. From the ridgepole the sides curve down and out to the ground, presenting a sloping surface to the wind at every angle. One corner can be lifted to cause a draft through the door and an open fire can be built in the tent without danger of suffocation from the smoke; moreover, it can be erected by a single person in ten minutes. We had an American wall tent also, but found it such a nuisance that we used it only during bad weather. In the wind which always blows upon the plains it flapped and fluttered to such a degree that we could hardly sleep.

As every traveler knows, the natives of a country usually have developed the best possible clothes and dwellings for the peculiar conditions under which they live. Just as the Mongol felt-covered *yurt* and tent are all that can be desired, so do they know that fur and leather are the only clothing to keep them warm during the bitter winter months.

In the carts we had an ample supply of flour, bacon, coffee, tea, sugar, and dried fruit. For meat, we depended upon our guns, of course, and always had as much as could be used. Although we did not travel *de luxe*, nevertheless we were entirely comfortable. When a man boasts of the way in which he discards even necessaries in the field, you can be morally certain that he has not done much real traveling. "Roughing it" does not harmonize well with hard work. One must accept enough discomforts under the best conditions without the addition of any which can be avoided. Good health is the prime requisite in the field. Without it you are lost. The only way in which to keep fit and ready to give every ounce of physical and mental energy to the problems of the day is to sleep comfortably, eat wholesome food, and be properly clothed. It is not often, then, that you will need a doctor. We have not as yet had a physician on any of our expeditions, even though we have often been very many miles from the nearest white men.

It never ceases to amuse me that the insurance companies always cancel my accident policies as soon as I leave for the field. The excuse is that I am not a "good risk," although they are ready enough to renew them when I return to New York. And yet the average person has a hundred times more chance of being killed or injured right on Fifth Avenue than do we who live in the open, breathing God's fresh air and sleeping under the stars. My friend Stefansson, the Arctic explorer, often says that "adventures are a mark of incompetence," and he is doubtless right. If a man goes into the field with a knowledge of the country he is to visit and with a proper equipment, he probably will have very few "adventures." If he has not the knowledge and equipment he had much better remain at home, for he will inevitably come to grief.

We learned from the Mongols that there was a wonderful shooting ground three hundred miles southwest of Urga in the country belonging to Sain Noin Khan. It was a region backed by mountains fifteen thousand feet in height, inhabited by bighorn sheep and ibex; and antelope were reported to be numerous upon the plains which merged gradually into the sandy wastes of the western Gobi where herds of wild horses (*Equus prjevalski*) and wild asses (*Equus hemionus*) could be found.

Sain Noin, one of the four Mongolian kings, had died only a short time earlier under suspicious circumstances, and his widow had just visited the capital. Monsieur Orlow, the Russian Diplomatic Agent, had written her regarding our prospective visit, and through him she had extended to us a cordial invitation.

Our start from Urga was on a particularly beautiful day, even for Mongolia. The golden roof of the great white temple on the hill blazed with light, and the undulating crest of the Sacred Mountain seemed so near that we imagined we could see the deer and boar in its parklike openings. Our way led across the valley and over the Tola River just below the palace of the Living God. We climbed a long hill and emerged on a sloping plain where marmots were bobbing in and out of their burrows like toy animals manipulated by a string. Two great flocks of demoiselle cranes were daintily catching grasshoppers not a hundred yards away. We wanted both the cranes for dinner and the marmots for specimens, but we dared not shoot. Although not actually upon sacred soil we were in close proximity to the Bogdo-ol and a rifle shot might have brought a horde of fanatical priests upon our heads. It is best to take no chances with religious superstitions, for the lamas do not wait to argue when they are once aroused.

The first day began most beautifully, but it ended badly as all first days are apt to do. We met our "Waterloo" on a steep hill shortly after tiffin, for two of the horses absolutely refused to pull. The loads were evidently too heavy, and the outlook for the future was not encouraging. An extract from my wife's journal tells what we did that afternoon.

"It took two hours to negotiate the hill, and the men were almost exhausted when the last load reached the summit. Ever since tiffin the sky had been growing darker and darker, and great masses of black clouds gathered about the crest of the Bogdo-ol. Suddenly a vivid flash of lightning cut the sky as though with a flaming knife, and the rain came down in a furious beat of icy water. In five minutes we were soaked and shivering with cold, so when at last we reached the plain we turned off the road toward two Mongol *yurts*, which rested beside the river a mile away like a pair of great white birds.

"Roy and I galloped ahead over the soft, slushy grass, nearly blinded by the rain, and hobbling our horses outside the nearest *yurt*, went inside with only the formality of a shout. The room was so dark that I could hardly see, and the heavy smoke from the open fire burned and stung our eyes. On the floor sat a frowzy-looking woman, blowing at the fire, and a yellow lama, his saucer hat hidden under its waterproof covering—apparently he was a traveler like ourselves.

"The frowzy lady smiled and motioned us to sit down on a low couch beside the door. As we did so, I saw a small face peering out of a big sheepskin coat and two black eyes staring at us unblinkingly. It was a little Mongol girl whose nap had been disturbed by so many visitors. She was rather a pretty little thing and so small—just a little older than my own baby in Peking—that I wanted to play with her. She was shy at first, but when I held out a picture advertisement from a package of cigarettes she gradually edged nearer, encouraged by her mother. Soon she was leaning on my knee. Then without taking her black eyes from my face, she solemnly put one finger in her mouth and jerked it out with a loud 'pop,' much to her mother's gratification. But when she decided to crawl up into my lap, my interest began to wane, for she exuded such a concentrated 'essence of Mongol' and rancid mutton fat that I was almost suffocated.

"Our hostess was busy stirring a thick, white soup in a huge cauldron, and by the time the carts arrived every one was dipping in with their wooden bowls. We begged to be excused, since we had already had some experience with Mongol soup.

"The *yurt* really was not a bad place when we became accustomed to the bitter smoke and the combination of native odors. There were two couches, about six inches from the ground, covered with sheepskins and furs. Opposite the door stood a chest—rather a nice one—on top of which was a tiny god with a candle burning before it, and a photograph of the Hutukhtu."

We had dinner in the *yurt,* and the boys slept there while we used our Mongol tent. There was no difficulty in erecting it even in the wind and rain, but it would have been impossible to have put up the American wall tent. Even though it was the fifth of June, there was a sharp frost during the night, and we were thankful for our fur sleeping bags.

Always in Mongolia after a heavy rain the air is crystal-clear, and we had a delightful morning beside the river. Hundreds of demoiselle cranes were feeding in the meadowlike valley bottom where the grass was as green as emeralds. We saw two of the graceful birds standing on a sand bar and, as we rode toward them, they showed not the slightest sign of fear. When we were not more than twenty feet away they walked slowly about in a circle, and the lama discovered two spotted brown eggs almost under his pony's feet. There was no sign of a nest, but the eggs were perfectly protected by their resemblance to the stones.

Our way led close along the Tola River, and just before

tiffin we saw a line of camels coming diagonally toward us from behind a distant hill. I wish you could have seen that caravan in all its barbaric splendor as it wound across the vivid green plains. Three lamas, dressed in gorgeous yellow robes, and two, in flaming red, rode ahead on ponies. Then neck and neck, mounted on enormous camels, came four men in gowns of rich maroon and a woman flashing with jewels and silver. Behind them, nose to tail, was the long, brown line of laden beasts. It was like a painting of the Middle Ages— like a picture of the days of Kublai Khan, when the Mongol court was the most splendid the world has ever seen. My wife and I were fascinated, for this was the Mongolia of our dreams.

But our second day was not destined to be one of unalloyed happiness, for just after luncheon we reached a bad stretch of road alternating between jagged rocks and deep mud holes. The white 'horse, which was so quickly exhausted the day before, gave up absolutely when its cart became badly mired. Just then a red lama appeared with four led ponies and said that one of his horses could extricate the cart. He hitched a tiny brown animal between the shafts, we all put our shoulders to the wheels, and in ten minutes the load was on solid ground. We at once offered to trade horses, and by giving a bonus of five dollars I became the possessor of the brown pony.

But the story does not end there. Two months later when we had returned to Urga a Mongol came to our camp in great excitement and announced that we had one of his horses. He said that five animals had been stolen from him and that the little brown pony for which I had traded with the lama was one of them. His proof was incontrovertible and according to the law of the country I was bound to give back the animal and accept the loss. However, a half dozen hard-riding Mongol soldiers at once took up the trail of the lama, and the chances are that there will be one less thieving priest before the incident is closed.

It is interesting to note how a similarity of conditions in western America and in Mongolia has developed exactly the same attitude of mutual protection in regard to horses. In both countries horse-stealing is considered to be one of the worst crimes. It is punishable by death in Mongolia or, what is infinitely worse, by a life in one of the prison coffins. Moreover, the spirit of mutual assistance is carried further, and several times during the summer when our ponies had strayed miles from the tents they were brought in by passing Mongols, or we were told where they could be found.

Our camp the second night was on a beautiful, grassy plateau beside a tiny stream, a tributary of the river. We put out a line of traps for small mammals, but in the morning were disappointed to find only three meadow mice (*Microtus*). There were no fresh signs of marmots, hares, or other animals along the river, and I began to suspect what eventually proved to be true, viz., that the valley was a favorite winter camping ground for Mongols, and that all the game had been killed or driven far away. Indeed, we had hardly been beyond sight of a *yurt* during the entire two days, and great flocks of sheep and goats were feeding on every grassy meadow.

But the Mongols considered cartridges too precious to waste on birds and we saw many different species. The demoiselle cranes were performing their mating dances all about us, and while one was chasing a magpie it made the most amusing spectacle, as it hopped and flapped after the little black and white bird which kept just out of reach.

Mongolian skylarks were continually jumping out of the grass from almost under our horses' feet to soar about our heads, flooding the air with song. Along the sand banks of the river we saw many flocks of swan geese (*Cygnopsis cygnoides*). They are splendid fellows with a broad, brown band down the back of the neck, and are especially interesting as being the ancestors of the Chinese domestic geese. They were not afraid of horses, but left immediately if a man on foot approached. I killed half a dozen by slipping off my pony, when about two hundred yards away, and walking behind the horses while Yvette rode boldly toward the flock, leading Kublai Khan. Twice the birds fell across the river, and we had to swim for them. My pony took to the water like a duck and when we had reached the other bank would arch his neck as proudly as though he had killed the bird himself. His keen interest in sport, his gentleness, and his intelligence won my heart at once. He would let me shoot from his back without the slightest fear, even though he had never been used as a hunting pony by Prince Tze Tze from whom he had been purchased.

In the ponds and among the long marsh grass we found the ruddy sheldrake (*Casarca casarca*), and the crested lapwing (*Vanellus vanellus*). They were like old friends, for we had met them first in far Yün-nan and on the Burma frontier during the winter of 1916-17 whence they had gone to escape the northern cold; now they were on their summer breeding grounds. The sheldrakes glowed like molten gold when the sun found them in the grass, and we could not have killed the beautiful birds even had we needed them for food. Moreover, like the lapwings, they had a trusting simplicity, a way of throwing themselves on one's mercy, which was infinitely appealing. We often hunted for the eggs of both the sheldrakes and lapwings. They must have been near by, we knew, for the old birds would fly about our heads uttering agonizing calls, but we never found the nests.

I killed four light-gray geese with yellow bills and legs and narrow brown bars across the head, and a broad brown stripe down the back of the neck. I could only identify the species as the bar-headed goose of India (*Eulabeia indica*), which I was not aware ever traveled so far north to breed. Later I found my identification to be correct, and that the bird is an occasional visitor to Mongolia. We saw only one specimen of the bean goose (*Anser fabalis*), the common bird of China, which I had expected would be there in thousands. There were a few mallards, redheads, and shoveler ducks, and several bustards, besides half a dozen species of plover and shore birds.

Except for these the trip would have been infinitely monotonous, for we were bitterly disappointed in the lack of animal life. Moreover, there was continual trouble with the carts, and on the third day I had to buy an extra horse. Although one can purchase a riding pony at any *yurt*, cart animals are not easy to find, for the Mongols use oxen or camels to draw most loads. The one we obtained had not been in the shafts for more than two years and was badly frightened when we brought him near the cart. It was a liberal education to see our Mongol handle that horse! He first put a hobble on all four legs, then he swung a rope about the hind quarters, trussed him tightly, and swung him into the shafts. When the pony was properly harnessed, he fastened the bridle to the rear of the other cart and drove slowly ahead. At first the horse tried to kick and plunge, but the hobbles held him fast and in fifteen minutes he settled to the work. Then the Mongol removed the hobbles from the hind legs, and later left the pony entirely free. He walked beside the animal for a long time, and did not attempt to drive him from the cart for at least an hour.

Although Mongols seem unnecessarily rough and almost brutal, I do not believe that any people in the world can handle horses more expertly. From earliest childhood their real home is the back of a pony. Every year, in the spring, a children's race is held at Urga. Boys and girls from four to six years old are tied on horses and ride at full speed over a mile-long course. If a child falls off it receives but scant sympathy and is strapped on again more tightly than before. A Mongol has no respect whatever for a man or woman who cannot ride, and nothing will win his regard as rapidly as expert horsemanship. Strangely enough the Mongols seldom show affection for their ponies, nor do they caress them in any way; consequently, the animals do not enjoy being petted and are prone to kick and bite. My pony, Kublai Khan, was an extraordinary exception to this rule and was as affectionate and gentle as a kitten—but there are few animals like Kublai Khan in Mongolia!

The ponies are small, of course, but they are strong almost beyond belief, and can stand punishment that would kill an ordinary horse. The Mongols seldom ride except at a trot or a full gallop, and forty to fifty miles a day is not an unusual journey. Moreover, the animals are not fed grain; they must forage on the plains the year round. During the winter, when the grass is dry and sparse, they have poor feeding, but nevertheless are able to withstand the extreme cold. They grow a coat of hair five or six inches in length, and when Kublai Khan arrived in Peking after his long journey across the plains he looked more like a grizzly bear than a horse. He had changed so completely from the sleek, fine-limbed animal we had known in Mongolia that my wife was almost certain he could not be the same pony. He had to be taught to eat carrots, apples, and other vegetables and would only sniff suspiciously at sugar. But in a very short time he learned all the tastes of his city-bred companions.

Horses are cheap in Mongolia, but not extraordinarily so. In the spring a fair pony can be purchased for from thirty to sixty dollars (silver), and especially good ones bring as much as one hundred and fifty dollars. In the fall when the Mongols are confronted with a hard winter, which naturally exacts a certain toll from any herd, ponies sell for about two-thirds of their spring price.

In Urga we had been led to believe that the entire trip to Sain Noin Khan's village could be done in eight days and that game was plentiful along the trail. We had already been on the road five days, making an average of twenty-five miles at each stage, and the natives assured us that it would require at least ten more days of steady travel before we could possibly arrive at our destination; if difficulties arose it might take even longer. Moreover, we had seen only one hare and one marmot, and our traps had yielded virtually nothing. It was perfectly evident that the entire valley had been denuded of animal life by the Mongols, and there was little prospect that conditions would change as long as we remained on such rich grazing grounds.

It was hard to turn back and count the time lost, but it was certainly the wisest course for we knew that there was good collecting on the plains south of Urga, although the fauna would not be as varied as at the place we had hoped to reach. The summer in Mongolia is so short that every day must be made to count if results which are worth the money invested are to be obtained.

Yvette and I were both very despondent that evening when we decided it was necessary to turn back. It was one of those nights when I wished with all my heart that we could sit in front of our own camp fire without the thought of having to "make good" to any one but ourselves. However, once the decision was made, we tried to forget the past days and determined to make up for lost time in the future.

PLATE VIII

The traffic policeman on Urga's "Broadway"

A Mongol Lama

The grasslands of outer Mongolia

CHAPTER VIII
THE LURE OF THE PLAINS

On Monday, June 16, we left Urga to go south along the old caravan trail toward Kalgan. Only a few weeks earlier we had skimmed over the rolling surface in motor cars, crossing in one day then as many miles of plains as our own carts could do in ten. But it had another meaning to us now, and the first night as we sat at dinner in front of the tent and watched the after-glow fade from the sky behind the pine-crowned ridge of the Bogdo-ol, we thanked God that for five long months we could leave the twentieth century with its roar and rush, and live as the Mongols live; we knew that the days of discouragement had ended and that we could learn the secrets of the desert life which are yielded up to but a chosen few.

Within twenty-five miles of Urga we had seen a dozen marmots and a species of gopher (*Citellus*) that was new to us. The next afternoon at two o'clock we climbed the last long slope from out the Tola River drainage basin, and reached the plateau which stretches in rolling waves of plain and desert to the frontier of China six hundred miles away. Before us three pools of water flashed like silver mirrors in the sunlight, and beyond them, tucked away in a sheltered corner of the hills, stood a little temple surrounded by a cluster of gray-white *yurts*.

Our Mongol learned that the next water was on the far side of a plain thirty-five miles in width, so we camped beside the largest pond. It was a beautiful spot with gently rolling hills on either side, and in front, a level plain cut by the trail's white line.

As soon as the tents were up Yvette and I rode off, accompanied by the lama, carrying a bag of traps. Within three hundred yards of camp we found the first marmot. When it had disappeared underground we carefully buried a steel trap at the entrance of the hole and anchored it securely to an iron tent peg. With rocks and earth we plugged all the other openings, for there are usually five or six tunnels to every burrow. While the work was going on other marmots were watching us curiously from half a dozen mounds, and we set nine traps before it was time to return for dinner.

The two Chinese taxidermists had taken a hundred wooden traps for smaller mammals, and before dark we inspected the places they had found. Already one of them held a gray meadow vole (*Microtus*), quite a different species from those which had been caught along the Tola River, and Yvette discovered one of the larger traps dragged halfway into a hole with a baby marmot safely caught. He was only ten inches long and covered with soft yellow-white fur.

Shortly after daylight the next morning the lama came to our tent to announce that there was a marmot in one of the traps. The boy was as excited as a child of ten and had been up at dawn. When we were dressed we followed the Mongol to the first burrow where a fine marmot was securely caught by the hind leg. A few yards away we had another female, and the third trap was pulled far into the hole. A huge male was at the other end, but he had twisted his body halfway around a curve in the tunnel and by pulling with all our strength the Mongol and I could not move him a single inch. Finally we gave up and had to dig him out. He had given a wonderful exhibition of strength for so small an animal.

It was especially gratifying to catch these marmots so easily, for we had been told in Urga that the Mongols could not trap them. I was at a loss to understand why, for they are closely related to the "woodchucks" of America with which every country boy is familiar. Later I learned the reason for the failure of the natives. In the Urga market we saw some double-spring traps exactly like those of ours, but when I came to examine them I found they had been made in Russia, and the springs were so weak that they were almost useless. These were the only steel traps which the Mongols had ever seen.

The marmots (*Marmota robusta*) were supposed to be responsible for the spread of the pneumonia plague which swept into northern China from Manchuria a few years ago; but I understand from physicians of the Rockefeller Foundation in Peking, who especially investigated the disease, that the animal's connection with it is by no means satisfactorily determined.

The marmots hibernate during the winter, and retire to

their burrows early in October, not to emerge until April. When they first come out in the spring their fur is bright yellow, and the animals contrast beautifully with the green grass. After the middle of June the yellow fur begins to slip off in patches, leaving exposed the new coat, which is exceedingly short and is mouse-gray in color. Then, of course, the skins are useless for commercial purposes. As the summer progresses the fur grows until by September first it has formed a long, soft coat of rich gray-brown which is of considerable economic value. The skins are shipped to Europe and America and during the past winter (1919-1920) were especially popular as linings for winter coats.

We had an opportunity to see how quickly the demand in the great cities reaches directly to the center of production thousands of miles away. When we went to Urga in May prime marmot skins were worth thirty cents each to the Mongols. Early in October, when we returned, the hunters were selling the same skins for *one dollar and twenty-jive cents apiece.*

The natives always shoot the animals. When a Mongol has driven one into its burrow, he lies quietly beside the hole waiting for the marmot to appear. It may be twenty minutes or even an hour, but the Oriental patience takes little note of time. Finally a yellow head emerges and a pair of shining eyes glance quickly about in every direction. Of course, they see the Mongol but he looks only like a mound of earth, and the marmot raises itself a few inches higher. The hunter lies as motionless as a log of wood until the animal is well put of its burrow—then he shoots.

The Mongols take advantage of the marmot's curiosity in an amusing and even more effective way. With a dogskin tied to his saddle the native rides over the plain until he reaches a marmot colony. He hobbles his pony at a distance of three or four hundred yards, gets down on his hands and knees, and throws the dogskin over his shoulders. He crawls slowly toward the nearest animal, now and then stopping to bark and shake his head. In an instant, the marmot is all attention. He jumps up and down whistling and barking, but never venturing far from the opening of his burrow.

As the pseudo-dog advances there seems imminent

danger that the fat little body will explode from curiosity and excitement. But suddenly the "dog" collapses in the strangest way and the marmot raises on the very tips of his toes to see what it is all about. Then there is a roar, a flash of fire and another skin is added to the millions which have already been sent to the sea-coast from outer Mongolia.

Mr. Mamen often spoke of an extraordinary dance which he had seen the marmots perform, and when Mr. and Mrs. MacCallie returned to Kalgan they saw it also. We were never fortunate enough to witness it. Mac said that two marmots stood erect on their hind legs, grasping each other with their front paws, and danced slowly about exactly as though they were waltzing. He agreed with Mamen that it was the most extraordinary and amusing thing he had ever seen an animal do. I can well believe it, for the marmots have many curious habits which would repay close study. The dance could hardly be a mating performance since Mac saw it in late May and by that time the young had already been born.

One morning at the "Marmot Camp," as we named the one where we first began real collecting, Yvette saw six or seven young animals on top of a mound in the green grass. We went there later with a gun and found the little fellows playing like kittens, chasing each other about and rolling over and over. It was hard to make myself bring tragedy into their lives, but we needed them for specimens. A group showing an entire marmot family would be interesting for the Museum; especially so in view of their reported connection with the pneumonic plague. We collected a dozen others before the summer was over to show the complete transition from the first yellow coat to the gray-brown of winter.

Like most rodents, the marmots grow rapidly and have so many young in every litter that they will not soon be exterminated in Mongolia unless the native hunters obtain American steel traps. Even then it would take some years to make a really alarming impression upon the millions which spread over all the plains of northern Mongolia and Manchuria.

Since these marmots are a distinctly northern animal they are a great help in determining the life zones of this part of

Asia. We found that their southern limit is at Turin, one hundred and seventy-five miles from Urga. A few scattered families live there, but the real marmot country begins about twenty-five miles farther north.

The first hunting camp was eighty miles south of Urga, after we had passed a succession of low hills and reached what, in prehistoric times, was probably a great lake basin. When our tents were pitched beside the well they seemed pitifully small in the vastness of the plain. The land rolled in placid waves to the far horizon on every hand. It was like a calm sea which is disturbed only by the lazy progress of the ocean swell. Two *yurts*, like the sails of hull-down ships, showed black against the sky-rim where it met the earth. The plain itself seemed at first as flat as a table, for the swells merged indistinguishably into a level whole. It was only when approaching horsemen dipped for a little out of sight and the depressions swallowed them up that we realized the unevenness of the land.

Camp was hardly made before our Mongol neighbors began to pay their formal calls. A picturesque fellow, blazing with color, would dash up to our tent at a full gallop, slide off and hobble his pony almost in a single motion. With a "*sai bina*" of greeting he would squat in the door, produce his bottle of snuff and offer us a pinch. There was a quiet dignity about these plains dwellers which was wonderfully appealing. They were seldom unduly curious, and when we indicated that the visit was at an end, they left at once.

Sometimes they brought bowls of curded milk, or great lumps of cheese as presents, and in return we gave cigarettes or now and then a cake of soap. Having been told in Urga that soap was especially appreciated by the Mongols, I had brought a supply of red, blue, and green cakes which had a scent even more wonderful than the color. I can't imagine why they like it, for it is carefully put away and never used.

Strangely enough, the Mongols have no word for "thank you" other than "*sai*" (good), but when they wish to express approbation, and usually when saying "good-by," they put up the thumb with the fingers closed. In Yün-nan and eastern Tibet we noted the same custom among the aboriginal tribesmen. I wonder if it is merely a coincidence that in the gladiatorial contests of ancient Rome "thumbs up" meant mercy or approval!

The Mongols told us that in the rolling ground to the east of camp we could surely find antelope. The first morning my wife and I went out alone. We trotted steadily for an hour, making for the summit of a rise seven or eight miles from camp. Yvette held the ponies, while I sat down to sweep the country with my glasses. Directly in front of us two small valleys converged into a larger one, and almost immediately I discovered half a dozen orange-yellow forms in its very bottom about two miles away. They were antelope quietly feeding. In a few moments I made out two more close together, and then four off at the right. After my wife had found them with her glasses we sat down to plan the stalk.

It was obvious that we should try to cross the two small depressions which debouched into the main valley and approach from behind the hill crest nearest to the gazelles. We trotted slowly across the gully while the antelope were in sight, and then swung around at full gallop under the protection of the rising ground. We came up just opposite to the herd and dismounted, but were fully six hundred yards away. Suddenly one of those impulses which the hunter never can explain sent them off like streaks of yellow light, but they turned on the opposite hillside, slowed down, and moved uncertainly up the valley.

Much to our surprise four of the animals detached themselves from the others and crossed the depression in our direction. When we saw that they were really coming we threw ourselves into the saddles and galloped forward to cut them off. Instantly the antelope increased their speed and literally flew up the hill slope. I shouted to Yvette to watch the holes and shook the reins over Kublai Khan's neck. Like a bullet he was off. I could feel his great muscles flowing between my knees but otherwise there seemed hardly a motion of his body in the long, smooth run. Standing straight up in the stirrups, I glanced back at my wife who was sitting her chestnut stallion as lightly as a butterfly. Hat gone, hair streaming, the thrill of it all showed in every line of her body. She was running a close second, almost at my side. I saw a marmot hole flash by. A second death trap showed ahead and

I swung Kublai Khan to the right. Another and another followed, but the pony leaped them like a cat. The beat of the fresh, clean air; the rush of the splendid horse; the sight of the yellow forms fleeing like wind-blown ribbons across our path—all this set me mad with excitement and a wild exhilaration. Suddenly I realized that I was yelling like an Indian. Yvette, too, was screaming in sheer delight.

The antelope were two hundred yards away when I tightened on the reins. Kublai Khan stiffened and stopped in twenty yards. The first shot was low and to the left, but it gave the range. At the second, the rearmost animal stumbled, recovered itself, and ran wildly about in a circle. I missed him twice, and he disappeared over a little hill. Leaping into the saddle, we tore after the wounded animal. As we thundered over the rise I heard my wife screaming frantically and saw her pointing to the right where the antelope was lying down. There was just one more shell in the gun and my pockets were empty. I fired again at fifty yards and the gazelle rolled over, dead.

Leading our horses, Yvette and I walked up to the beautiful orange-yellow form lying in the fresh, green grass. We both saw its horns in the same instant and hugged each other in sheer delight. At this time of the year the bucks are seldom with the does and then only in the largest herds. This one was in full pelage, spotless and with the hair unworn. Moreover, it had finer horns than any other which we killed during the entire trip.

Kublai Khan looked at the dead animal and arched his neck, as much as to say, "Yes, I ran him down. He had to quit when I really got started." My wife held the pony's head, while I hoisted the antelope to his back and strapped it behind the saddle. He watched the proceedings interestedly but without a tremor, and even when I mounted, he paid not the slightest attention to the head dangling on his flanks. Thereby he showed that he was a very exceptional pony. In the weeks which followed he proved it a hundred times, and I came to love him as I have never loved another animal.

Yvette and I trotted slowly back to camp, thrilled with the excitement of the wild ride. We began to realize that we were lucky to have escaped without broken necks. The race taught us never again to attempt to guide our ponies away from the marmot holes which spotted the plains, for the horses could see them better than we could and all their lives had known that they meant death.

That morning was our initiation into what is the finest sport we have ever known. Hunting from a motor car is undeniably exciting at first, but a real sportsman can never care for it very long. The antelope does not have a chance against gas and steel and a long-range rifle. On horseback the conditions are reversed. An antelope can run twice as fast as the best horse living. It can see as far as a man with prism binoculars. All the odds are in the animal's favor except two—its fatal desire to run in a circle about the pursuer, and the use of a high-power rifle. But even then an antelope three hundred yards away, going at a speed of fifty miles an hour, is not an easy target.

Of course, the majority of sportsmen will say that it cannot be done with any certainty—until they go to Mongolia and do it themselves! But, as I remarked in a previous chapter, conditions on the plains are so unusual that shooting in other parts of the world is no criterion. After one gets the range of an animal which, like the antelope, has a smooth, even run, it is not so difficult to hit as one might imagine. Practice is the great essential. At the beginning I averaged one antelope to every eight cartridges, but later my score was one to three.

We spent the afternoon at the new camp, setting traps and preparing for the days to come—days in which we knew, from long experience, we would have every waking moment full of work. The nights were shortening rapidly, and the sun did not dip below the rim of our vast, flat world until half past seven. Then there was an hour of delightful, lingering twilight, when the stars began to show in tiny points of light; by nine o'clock the brooding silence of the Mongolian night had settled over all the plain.

Daylight came at four o'clock, and before the sun rose we had finished breakfast. Our traps held five marmots and a beautiful golden-yellow polecat (*Mustela*). I have never seen such an incarnation of fury as this animal presented. It might have been the original of the Chinese dragon, except for its small size. Its long, slender body twisted and turned with incredible swiftness, every hair was bristling, and its snarling little face emitted horrible squeaks and spitting squeals. It seemed to be cursing us in every language of the polecat tribe.

The fierce little beast was evidently bent upon a night raid on a marmot family. We could imagine easily into what terror the tiny demon would throw a nest of marmots comfortably snuggled together in the bottom of their burrow. Probably it would be most interested in the babies, and undoubtedly would destroy every one within a few moments. All the weasel family, to which the polecat belongs, kill for the pure joy of killing, and in China one such animal will entirely depopulate a hen-roost in a single night.

At six o'clock Yvette and I left camp with the lama and rode northeast. The plain swept away in long, grassy billows, and at every rise I stopped for a moment to scan the horizon with my glasses. Within half an hour we discovered a herd of antelope six or seven hundred yards away. They saw us instantly and trotted nervously about, staring in our direction.

Dropping behind the crest of the rise, I directed the lama to ride toward them from behind while we swung about to cut them off. He was hardly out of sight when we heard a snort and a rush of pounding hoofs. With a shout to Yvette I loosened the reins over Kublai Khan's neck, and he shot forward like a yellow arrow. Yvette was close beside me, leaning far over her pony's neck. We headed diagonally toward the herd, and they gradually swung toward us as though drawn by a powerful magnet. On we went, down into a hollow and up again on its slope. We could not spare the horses for the antelope were already over the crest and lost to view, but our horses took the hill at full speed, and from the summit we could see the herd fairly on our course, three hundred yards away.

Kublai Khan braced himself like a polo pony when he felt the pressure of my knees, and I opened fire almost under his nose. At the crack of the rifle there was a spurt of brown dust near the leading animal. "High and to the left," shouted Yvette, and I held a little lower for the second trial. The antelope dropped like a piece of white paper, shot through the neck. I paced the distance and found it to be three hundred and sixty-seven yards. It seemed a very long shot then, but later I found that almost none of my antelope were killed at less than three hundred yards.

As I came up to Kublai Khan with the dead animal, I accidentally struck him on the flank with my rifle in such a way that he was badly frightened. He galloped off, and Yvette had a hard chase before he finally allowed her to catch him. Had I been alone I should probably have had a long walk to camp.

It taught us never to hunt without a companion, if it could possibly be avoided. If your horse runs away, you may be left many miles from water, with rather serious consequences. I think there is nothing which makes me feel more helpless than to be alone on the plains without a horse. For miles and miles there is only the rolling grassland or the wide sweep of desert, with never a house or tree to break the low horizon. It seems so futile to walk, your own legs carry you so slowly and such a pitifully short distance, in these vast spaces.

To be left alone in a small boat on the open sea is exactly similar. You feel so very, very small and you realize then what an insignificant part of nature you really are. I have felt it, too, amid vast mountains when I have been toiling up a peak which stretched thousands of feet above me with others rearing their majestic forms on every side. Then, nature seems almost alive and full of menace; something to be fought and conquered by brain and will.

Early in our work upon the plains we learned how easy it is to lose one's way. The vast sea of land seems absolutely flat, but in reality it is a gently rolling surface full of slopes and hollows, every one of which looks exactly like the others. But after a time we developed a *land sense*. The Mongols all have it to an extraordinary degree. We could drop an antelope on the plain and leave it for an hour or more. With a quick glance about our lama would fix the place in his mind, and dash off on a chase which might carry us back and forth toward every point of the compass. When it was time to return, he would head his pony unerringly for that single spot on the plain and take us back as straight as the flight of an arrow.

At first it gave him unceasing enjoyment when we became

completely lost, but in a very short time we learned to note the position of the sun, the character of the ground, and the direction of the wind. Then we began to have more confidence in ourselves. But only by years of training can one hope even to approximate the Mongols. They have been born and reared upon the plains, and have the inheritance of unknown generations whose very life depended upon their ability to come and go at will. To them, the hills, the sun, the grass, the sand—all have become the street signs of the desert.

In the afternoon of our second day I remained at the tents to measure specimens, while Yvette and the lama rode out toward the scene of our morning hunt to locate an antelope which one of our Mongol neighbors had reported dead not far away. At six o'clock they came galloping back with the news that there were two gazelles within three miles of camp. I saddled Kublai Khan and left with them at once. Twenty minutes of steady trotting brought us to the summit of a slope, where we could see the animals quietly feeding not five hundred yards away.

It was just possible to stalk them for a long-range shot, and slipping off my pony, I flattened out upon the ground. On hands and knees, and sometimes at full length, I wormed my way through the grass for one hundred yards. The cover ended there and I must shoot or come into full view of the gazelles. They were so far away that the front sight entirely covered the animals, and to increase the difficulty, both were walking slowly. The first bullet struck low and to the right, but the antelope only jumped and stared fixedly in my direction; at the second shot one went down. The other animal dashed away like a flash of lightning, and although I sent a bullet after its white rump-patch, the shot was hopeless.

The antelope I had knocked over got to its feet and tried desperately to get away, but the lama leaped on his pony and caught it by one hind leg. My automatic pistol was not in working order, and it was necessary to knife the poor beast— a job which I hate like poison. The lama walked away a dozen yards and covered his face with the sleeve of his gown. It is against the laws of the Buddhist religion to take the life of any animal or even to see it done, although there are no restrictions as to eating flesh.

With a blanket the Mongol made a seat for himself on his pony's haunches, and threw the antelope across his saddle; then we trotted back to camp into the painted western sky, with the cool night air bringing to us the scent of newborn grass. We would not have exchanged our lot that night with any one on earth.

CHAPTER IX
HUNTING ON THE TURIN PLAIN

After ten days we left the "Antelope Camp" to visit the Turin plain where we had seen much game on the way to Urga. One by one our Mongol neighbors rode up to say "farewell," and each to present us with a silk scarf as a token of friendship and good will. We received an invitation to stop for tea at the *yurt* of an old man who had manifested an especial interest in us, but it was a very dirty *yurt*, and the preparations for tea were so uninviting that we managed to exit gracefully before it was finally served.

Yvette photographed the entire family including half a dozen dogs, a calf, and two babies, much to their enjoyment. When we rode off, our hands were heaped with cheese and slabs of mutton which were discarded as soon, as we had dropped behind a slope. Mongol hospitality is whole-souled and generously given, but one must be very hungry to enjoy their food.

A day and a half of traveling was uneventful, for herds of sheep and horses indicated the presence of *yurts* among the hills. Game will seldom remain where there are Mongols. Although it was the first of July, we found a heavy coating of ice on the lower sides of a deep well. The water was about fifteen feet below the level of the plain, and the ice would probably remain all summer. Moreover, it is said that the wells never freeze even during the coldest winter.

The changes of temperature were more rapid than in any other country in which I have ever hunted. It was hot during the day—about 85° Fahrenheit—but the instant the sun disappeared we needed coats, and our fur sleeping bags were always acceptable at night.

We were one hundred and fifty miles from Urga and were still going slowly south, when we had our next real hunting camp. Great bands of antelope were working northward from the Gobi Desert to the better grazing on the grass-covered Turin plain. We encountered the main herd one evening about six o'clock, and it was a sight which made us gasp for breath. We were shifting camp, and my wife and I were trotting along parallel to the carts which moved slowly over the trail a mile away. We had had a delightful, as well as a profitable, day. Yvette had been busy with her camera, while I picked up an antelope, a bustard, three hares, and half a dozen marmots. We were loafing in our saddles, when suddenly we caught sight of the cook standing on his cart frantically signaling us to come.

PLATE IX

Mongol herdsmen carrying lassos

A lone camp on the desert

In ten seconds our ponies were flying toward the caravan, while we mentally reviewed every accident which possibly could have happened to the boys. Lü met us twenty yards from the trail, trembling with excitement and totally incoherent. He could only point to the south and stammer, "Too many antelope. Over there. Too many, too many."

I slipped off Kublai Khan's back and put up the glasses. Certainly there were animals, but I thought they must be sheep or ponies. Hundreds were in sight, feeding in one vast herd and in many smaller groups. Then I remembered that the nearest well was twenty miles away; therefore they could not be horses. I looked again and knew they must be antelope—not in hundreds, but in thousands.

Mr. Larsen in Urga had told us of herds like this, but we had never hoped to see one. Yet there before us, as far as the eye could reach, was a yellow mass of moving forms. In a moment Yvette and I had left the carts. There was no possibility of concealment, and our only chance was to run the herd. When we were perhaps half a mile away the nearest animals threw up their heads and began to stamp and run about, only to stop again and stare at us. We kept on very slowly, edging nearer every moment. Suddenly they decided that we were really dangerous, and the herd strung out like a regiment of yellow-coated soldiers.

Kublai Khan had seen the antelope almost as soon as we left the carts, and although he had already traveled forty miles that day, was nervously champing the bit with head up and ears erect. When at last I gave him the word, he gathered himself for one terrific spring; down went his head and he dashed forward with every ounce of strength behind his flying legs. His run was the long, smooth stride of a thoroughbred, and it sent the blood surging through my veins in a wild thrill of exhilaration. Once only I glanced back at Yvette. She was almost at my side. Her hair had loosened and was flying back like a veil behind her head. Tense with excitement, eyes shining, she was heedless of everything save those skimming yellow forms before us. It was useless to look for holes; ere I had seen one we were over or around it. With head low down and muzzle out, my pony needed not the slightest touch to guide him. He knew where we were going and the part he had to play.

More than a thousand antelope were running diagonally across our course. It was a sight to stir the gods; a thing to give one's life to see. But when we were almost near enough to shoot, the herd suddenly swerved heading directly away from us. In an instant we were enveloped in a whirling cloud